Write from the Start

Ann B. Loomis

Discover Your Writing Potential through the Power of Psychological Type

Published by
Center for Applications of Psychological Type
2815 N.W. 13th Street, Suite 401
Gainesville, Florida 32609
(352) 375-0160

The publisher greatly acknowledges Beatrice Smyder
for the cover design and layout of this book.

Printed in the United States of America.

ISBN 0-935652-49-3

Table of Contents

Foreword: by Margaret T. Hartzler, Ph.D.

"Write from the Start" is a much needed, practical book on how to make writing work easier while at the same time producing higher quality results. Ann Loomis does this by using personality type and brain hemisphere theories to describe the natural gifts and potential trouble spots of different people. Other books have done this, but what makes this book so valuable is the abundance of tools, examples, and techniques you can apply to make your writing process produce successful products.

Reading this book brought back some painful memories for me. As an elementary and high school student, I was one of those persons who did not like to write. This distaste for writing influenced me to major in math in college. I did not have to write one paper for any of the courses in my major! What a relief, but also what a price I paid. In my junior year I was sent to a remedial writing course by a humanities professor. I had to attend and pass this course or not graduate. Think of the feelings of incompetence and embarrassment that I could have avoided if some teacher had used ideas from or given me a book like this to help me identify my preferred style and given me many possible ways to approach writing.

For those of you who don't particularly like to write but are required to, working with the ideas in this book will make your job easier – and you may even start to enjoy writing.

For those of you who like to write, you will find many ideas on how to make your writing more appealing to people who are very different from you. At the same time, it will give you renewed confidence that your style needs to be honored even when others are trying to tell you to do it their way.

By taking the Writing Inventory, you can get some ideas about your preferred writing process. Next, you can read how this style will probably play out in the four stages of the writing process. To get the maximum benefit from this book, you should practice the specific techniques described for each stage. By studying the before and after in the examples, you can experience the excitement of seeing how these techniques can really improve a piece of writing.

My hope is that every school in this country will have a copy of "Write from the Start." That teachers will read it so they can help students work from their natural style and not force them to write in a prescribed style. That adults will use it in improving the writing they have to do for work and in helping their children develop their writing talents. That young students will find it fun to write using the exercises offered. And most of all, that people who read this book will find out more about who they are as persons and how they can more effectively relate to themselves and others.

Preface: by Ann B. Loomis

Write from the Start
Discover Your Writing Style Through Psychological Type

I first became interested in using "type to write" in 1990 when I taught a three-day workshop called "Developing Writing Confidence" for a government agency in Washington, DC. Not having designed the workshop, I taught it the way the designer intended, with only one day devoted to using personality type to help participants go through the writing process. After teaching this workshop several times, I was convinced that understanding personality type is a valid step towards developing writing confidence. Writing using type affirms the value of individual style and helps reduce writer's anxiety.

An integral part of the workshop material was an article by John K. DiTiberio and George H. Jensen titled "Personality and Individual Writing Processes." DiTiberio and Jensen, both professors of composition at the college level, have conducted research on the link between personality type and writing style. They believe that students write with less anxiety if they begin with their preferred mental processes and revise from their less preferred processes (4: pp. 285-297).

When I moved to Chapel Hill, North Carolina, in 1992, Daniel Grandstaff and I decided to pursue this idea. We designed an eight-week course for Duke University's Continuing Education Program in Durham, NC. As a structure for the course, we drew on Betty S. Flower's article, "Madman, Architect, Carpenter, Judge: Roles and the Writing Process" (7: pp. 834-836). Her work inspired our comparison of the stages of the writing process to the stages of building a house. This workbook continues and expands that comparison.

In designing our course, we also drew on current brain research. Information on the right and left brain hemispheres convinced us that writer's block occurs most often when the left brain hemisphere dominates in the first two stages of the writing process. This workbook builds on the idea of allowing the right brain hemisphere to create before bringing in the left hemisphere to critique.

The response to our workshop at Duke was overwhelmingly positive. Meanwhile, we were further encouraged by the publication of DiTiberio and Jensen's book, *Writing and Personality: Finding Your Voice, Your Style, Your Way* (5). This book provides a fine model for illustrating the link between personality type and writing style. DiTiberio and Jensen make the complex issue of type more understandable to a general audience.

This workbook complements their book by offering many interactive exercises. The approach is primarily "how-to," frequently using the second person pronoun "you." The techniques suggested are all type specific, and learning is reinforced with illustrations and writing samples.

How This Book is Organized

This book is divided into three sections. Section I, "Personality Type and Writing Style," includes Chapters One and Two. Chapter One, "Understanding Type," explains the concepts behind type and shows how type and writing are linked. It also looks at current brain research. Chapter Two, "The Writing Profiles," gives a general description of the different types and their writing styles.

Section II, "The Four Stages of the Writing Process," includes Chapters Three through Ten. Chapters Three and Four discuss the first stage, "The Dreamer." Chapters Five and Six cover the second stage, "The Designer." Chapters Seven and Eight explore the third stage, "The Builder," and Chapters Nine and Ten conclude the writing process with stage four, "The Inspector."

Section III, "Continuing to Grow as a Writer," includes Chapters Eleven and Twelve. Chapter

Eleven is a compilation of writing samples from professional writers. Chapter Twelve, "WriteType: Putting it all Together," helps to answer lingering questions about type and the writing process. In the back of the workbook is an appendix of additional material to use in the revising stage.

How to Use This Book

Section One: Personality Type and Writing Style

You might want to take the Myers-Briggs Type Indicator (MBTI®) before you read this book so that reading it doesn't "prejudice" your responses. If you decide not to take the MBTI, you can probably figure out your type by carefully going through Chapter One. If you have already taken the MBTI, read the information in this chapter to confirm your type. Once you have determined your type, take the Loomis-Grandstaff Writing Inventory. Your score on the Inventory should be the same as your MBTI type; a different score may indicate some areas causing writing difficulties.

Chapter Two is a set of profiles with a general description of each personality type and each type's writing style. The information in the profiles draws on the link between current brain research and current type research. You can use the profiles to continue determining your type or to confirm your type.

Section Two: The Four Stages of the Writing Process

Chapter Three begins a discussion of the first stage of the writing process, the Dreamer. In this chapter, I invite you to look closely at your writing habits and open your mind to new ways of gathering information. Even though some of the techniques suggested here will appeal to you more than other techniques, be sure not to judge them before you try them.

Chapter Four shows you how to use your preferences in the Dreamer Stage. For each type, I've included a list of "tendencies" and "troublespots" followed by "tools to try." Look up your type and try some of the tools. They should help reduce anxiety associated with a blank page or computer screen. Remember that the main idea of this workbook is to start writing from your preferences and your tendencies.

Chapter Five introduces the second stage of the writing process, the Designer. Like the Dreamer, the Designer is part of creating your piece — the difference is that you are now ready to find theme and order. In this stage, you'll think about how to organize your piece. However, you are still free to gather information in the Designer Stage.

Chapter Six follows much the same format as Chapter Four: look up your type and try some of the tools suggested. Remember that you are still writing from your preferences, so try not to let your "inner critic" intrude. If you find yourself starting to judge your writing, concentrate on silencing the inner critic.

Chapter Seven explores the third stage of the writing process, the Builder. This chapter suggests ways to improve your content by using such techniques as anecdotes, examples, and definitions. You may have already used some of these techniques in your first drafts when you were generating ideas. This chapter shows you how to develop your draft more fully by considering many different ways to build content and to relate to your audience.

Chapter Eight shows you how to use your less preferred processes when you are fleshing out your piece in the Builder Stage. Since the differences between sensing and intuition can result in the greatest communication problems, I offer tips for bridging that gap. This chapter also focuses on the differences between thinking and feeling so that value judgments will be better accepted by other types. I stress the importance of doing the exercises in this chapter because practice is the best way to strengthen your less preferred processes.

Chapter Nine introduces the fourth stage, the Inspector. This chapter involves writing clear paragraphs and sentences and selecting the best word to convey your intended meaning. At this point, it is finally time to allow your inner critic to give you feedback on the details that make for a polished product.

Chapter Ten offers tips for getting a good start on the revising stage by using your preferred processes. Since looking at whole type is often more useful than looking at the individual scales, I encourage you to write a "prescription" for your type to use when revising. Writing a prescription for your opposite type should help you bring in your less preferred processes in the Inspector Stage to give you a more complete checklist for revising.

Section Three: Continuing to Grow as a Writer

This section gives you further insight into the implications of learning how to use type to write. The professional writing samples in Chapter Eleven offer opportunities to practice writing like the masters. By going through the samples and doing the exercises, you can get a better idea of what makes up an effective piece of writing.

Chapter Twelve, "WriteType: Putting it all Together," looks at type dynamics and the stages of type development. It gives suggestions for continuing to improve your writing as you grow in your understanding of type. As you go through this chapter, think about how your own writing process has affected your experience with writer's block.

The "Sentence Pattern Sheet" in the appendix is for anyone who needs further work with sentence variety, clarity of expression, and punctuation. I also include a list of active verbs to help you enliven your prose. The suggested books and software should be helpful resources for increasing your knowledge of both writing and type.

You can use this workbook to strengthen your own writing skills, to help students in the classroom, or to improve communication skills in businesses and organizations. But above all, enjoy your journey through the workbook. May it help build self-awareness, reawaken your imagination, and light your creative spark!

Acknowledgments

Many people helped bring this book to fruition in many different ways. To all the friends, colleagues, and family members who encouraged and supported me, I am deeply grateful. I wish I could mention all of you.

The ones that I do mention have contributed their time and talents in very specific ways.

- Dan Grandstaff, friend and colleague, supported the idea of this workbook right from the start. Without his time and encouragement, the workbook would probably still be in the dreamer stage. I would particularly like to thank him for co-authoring the Writing Inventory and for providing guidance on Chapter Five, "The Designer." Dan also contributed the writing sample, "Reducing Holiday Stress."

- Margaret Hartzler, of Type Resources, lent her expertise on type in the final stages of this project. Her editing showed me ways to make "type talk" more understandable. Encouragement from Margaret was uplifting at a crucial time in this project. I would also like to thank her for writing the foreword to this book.

- Tom Thompson, a member of the Editorial Board at CAPT, edited the final manuscript in a timely and professional manner. Since Tom has used type in composition classes, he was able to pinpoint places in the manuscript that might be confusing to students. His tips on clarity of expression were especially helpful.

- Bella English, a columnist for *The Boston Globe* (and also my cousin), read the manuscript when it was about halfway through completion. As a professional writer, Bella was able to make stylistic suggestions that helped guide the tone for the rest of the manuscript. I also thank Bella for sharing her articles "Who's Watching the Children?" and "Blame Game Hits New Low" for Chapter Eleven.

- Karen Ridout, past president of our local chapter of The Association for Psychological Type (APT), also read the manuscript at its halfway mark. Her encouragement and enthusiasm not only buoyed my spirits but also reinforced my faith in this project. Her "keep going" attitude propelled me forward. I thank all my friends from APT who have been enthusiastic about this project.

- Carol Shumate, friend and colleague, participated in my writing workshop and then told me, "Write that workbook!" Without our conversations, I might not have. I also thank Carol for contributing the writing sample, "Carmen."

- I thank all the participants in my writing workshops, but especially Al Thompson, who contributed the writing sample, "The Blue Rock."

- Ruth Hamilton and Mary Charles Blakebrough, support group friends, listened to my "venting" sessions with humor, creativity, and vision.

- And special thanks to my spouse, Bob Loomis, who lent his ear during several periods of anxiety and doubt. His steady encouragement and "can do" attitude spurred me on during times of stress, including "computer distress." I especially appreciated his very practical help around the house when a deadline loomed. Bob contributed the writing sample, "Critters."

Dedication

I dedicate this book to my mother, Lillian S. Buie, who was my first writing teacher. She affirmed my early attempts to express myself and, when I was ready, gently led me towards more creative ways to grow as a writer.

I also dedicate this book (posthumously) to Flora Steele, my high school English teacher, who always gave me A's for writing my natural way.

Section One:

Personality Type and Writing Style

Introduction

The Myers-Briggs Type Indicator®

The seeds for the Myers-Briggs Type Indicator® (MBTI®) were planted by the Swiss psychologist Carl Jung (1875-1961). His pivotal work on type, *Psychological Types* (1923), focused on three pairs of opposite processes: extraversion and introversion, sensing and intuition, and thinking and feeling.

Extraversion and introversion are about energy flow. People who prefer extraversion are usually energized by the outer world of people and objects. People who prefer introversion usually need to recharge their energy by turning to their inner world.

Sensing and intuition are processes for gathering and perceiving information. People who prefer the sensing perception tend to trust information that comes from the five senses. They perceive the information "as is" and tend to take it at face value. People who prefer the intuitive perception look at patterns and nuances that underlie "what is" and gather information that goes beyond the five senses.

Thinking and feeling are processes for making decisions on the information we gather. People who prefer the thinking judgment are more comfortable making decisions by analyzing impersonal and objective data. People who prefer the feeling judgment like to consider values that are formed by personal and subjective data when they make decisions.

When Katharine Briggs and her daughter, Isabel Myers, designed the MBTI in the early 1940's, they added the opposite pairs of judging and perceiving to Jung's theory of personality type. Judging and perceiving have to do with how we deal with the outer world. People who prefer judging are more comfortable with plans, schedules, structure, and getting to closure. People who prefer perceiving like to provide their own structure to build in flexibility and spontaneity. They like to stay open to new information and options.

The MBTI is a series of forced-choice questions and word pairs designed to sort preferences on extraversion/introversion, sensing/intuition, thinking/feeling, and judging/perceiving. Our preferences can help predict how we choose our careers, how we choose our mates, and how we like to live our lives.

Millions of people in the U.S. and around the world have taken the MBTI for personal and professional development. Its application to learning and writing styles is just beginning to be explored. I believe that the MBTI is an ideal instrument for helping to tap writing potential because its emphasis on preferences avoids claiming that one approach to writing is better than another approach.

Type and Writing

Take yourself back to your earliest writing experiences. Since learning to write was a new skill, it may have been exciting or traumatic, depending on how it was taught. If it was a positive experience, you may have delighted in self-expression and the joy of seeing your thoughts on paper. Your teacher may have praised you for your creative ideas, and you felt that writing was nothing to fear. But as you progressed through school, your teachers began to offer their insight into what made up "good writing," and that usually meant writing their way.

Perhaps they wanted you to make an outline, or be more objective, or insert more feeling into the piece, or use figurative language, or write more dialogue. The advice was no doubt endless. By that time, you were either totally confused or turned off – and you left high school or college vowing to let a secretary or a colleague handle your writing tasks.

Now, thanks to Carl Jung's insights on preferences, we know that people are innately different, with different interests and ways of looking at the world. If not allowed to be ourselves, we often feel uncreative and blocked. The same is true of writing – if we are not allowed to write from our own personality, we encounter blocks and feel depleted rather than energized.

A friend once told me of her experience writing her dissertation. Her directing professor was structured and organized with an affinity for facts, which he considered indisputable. My friend tried valiantly to please this professor, but all the while she felt her writing was forced, lifeless. Then one day all her notes mysteriously disappeared – every draft she had written was gone. Desperate, she began from scratch, trying to recall from memory what she had written since she didn't have the benefit of a computer in those days. With great chagrin, she turned in her new draft to the professor, who was surprised to find her writing greatly improved.

After taking the workshop on the link between personality type and writing style, my friend offered this insight: "When I was writing for my professor, I couldn't please him. I followed his instructions to the letter, but my writing ended up sounding like a false version of him – stilted style, faulty logic, and forced transitions. When in desperation I wrote like myself, I ended up pleasing him." Since my friend's personality type was ENFP, we concluded that the professor's type was probably ISTJ or something close.

ENFP? ISTJ? For readers unfamiliar with "type talk," Chapter One explains the four letters that make up type. Even if you have taken the Myers-Briggs Type Indicator, go through this chapter to help reinforce your understanding of type – and to confirm your own.

Chapter One:
Understanding Type

Some people resist the idea of type because they don't want to be put into a category or a "box." They may say that no type or profile fits them perfectly, or that they know someone of their type who isn't like them at all, or that they have "changed type" over the years.

Psychological type doesn't put us into a box; it sorts us according to our innate tendencies and preferences. Once we understand what they are, we can more easily channel them in productive ways. We can also grow within type (not change type) as we learn how to integrate the tendencies and preferences of other personality types. And no two people are the same within type because we are all unique individuals with different environments and experiences.

Keep in mind as you read over the four pairs of opposites that we all have some characteristics of both extraversion and introversion, sensing and intuition, thinking and feeling, and judging and perceiving. The key is to choose the one that you prefer.

Extraversion and Introversion: The Attitudes

Carl Jung called extraversion and introversion "attitudes" to talk about energy flow. People whose energy flows outward prefer the extraverted attitude while people whose energy flows inward prefer the introverted attitude.

Parents report that they see characteristics of extraversion and introversion in very young children – one child will be into everything while his or her sibling will quietly observe before jumping into activities. Environment may affect how we show our extraversion or introversion, but the preference will always be there.

Look at the descriptors under each of the sets and select the descriptors that best fit who you are. When you are done, look to see if there is one set of descriptors that better describes the way you have been for most of your life, not just the way you are now. For example, if you are in mid-life, you may have a need for more solitude. Consider, instead, the overall pattern of your life. When you have chosen the set you prefer, circle the word (either Extraversion or Introversion) at the top of the set.

EXTRAVERSION (E)	INTROVERSION (I)
Attention focused on things and objects and/or people	Attention focused on inner impressions/ideas
Prefers to act	Prefers to reflect
Talks to understand	Listens to internal messages
Stimulated by social events	Energized by being alone
Breadth of interests	Depth of interests
Open	Private
Group interaction	One-on-one interaction
Likes to know many people	Prefers close friendships

Sensing and Intuition: The Perceiving Functions

The sensing function is easy to understand because most everybody gathers information (or perceives) through the five senses. But people who prefer the sensing function rely on the five senses more than people who prefer the intuitive function. Sensing types like to get involved with real-life situations and to see concrete results. They believe in and trust as real what they are experiencing or have experienced.

Intuitive types use a sixth sense to perceive the world through hunches, patterns, and undertones. It is as though intuitive types have a "third eye" that sees symbolically. People who prefer intuition like to explore implications, to improve on the status quo, or to offer a new solution. They trust possibilities and theories perhaps even more than experience.

Look at the descriptors under the sets below and choose the set that better describes your preferences. Again, choose the set that you have felt more comfortable with most of your life. When you have selected your preferred set, circle the word at the top. (Intuition is marked by an N so that it won't be confused with introversion.)

SENSING (S)	INTUITION (N)
Cites facts	Connects facts
Sees details	Sees big picture
Notes what is	Notes what could be
Goes by experience	Goes on hunches
Present or past	Future or present
Practical	Ingenious
Literal	Figurative
Concrete	Abstract
Sequential or contextual	Patterns

Thinking and Feeling: The Judging Functions

We use thinking and feeling to evaluate or come to closure about the information we've perceived. Thinking and feeling types generally like to come to closure in different ways. Their decision-making process is usually based on either objectivity (thinking) or subjectivity (feeling).

Let's say that a thinking type mother and a feeling type father are trying to decide whether or not to let their 16-year-old daughter go to an unchaperoned party where there will be alcohol. The thinking type mother wants to let the daughter go because "How else is she to learn responsibility?" The feeling type father also wants to let the daughter go because "How would I feel if I had my heart set on the party and my parents changed their minds about letting me go?"

Or the parents decide not to let their daughter go. The thinking type mother says, "I am the parent, and it's my responsibility to protect my daughter." The feeling type father says, "What matters most is that our daughter knows we care about what happens to her." Whether or not the daughter goes to the party, the parents go about their decision-making process based on different values.

Now look at the descriptors under each set and decide how you prefer to come to decisions. When you have selected the set you feel more comfortable with, circle the word at the top.

THINKING (T)	FEELING (F)
Principles	Circumstances
Objective	Subjective
Justice	Mercy
Logical analysis	Compassion or empathy
Critique	Appreciate
Firm	Gentle
Categorize	Harmonize
Convince	Persuade
Reasonable	Personable

Judging and Perceiving: The Orientation to Outer World

Judging does not mean judgmental; it means that, when dealing with the outside world, you like to bring things to closure. Judging types are usually oriented toward a structured and ordered lifestyle and like to plan ahead. They "extravert" (or show to the world) their judging function (either thinking or feeling) and therefore tend to sound certain and definite.

Perceiving types extravert (show to the world) their perceiving function (either sensing or intuition), which is the function that likes to gather information. They prefer a more flexible lifestyle than judging types and like to keep options open. They may sound more tentative than "final."

Look over the descriptors in each set for the words or phrases that most appeal to you. If you are in a job that requires a lot of structure, be sure to consider whether or not you feel comfortable with that structure. Examine your real needs when you are considering which set to choose, and then circle the word at the top.

JUDGING (J)	PERCEIVING (P)
Likes closure	Likes options open
Plans events ahead	Lets events happen
Scheduled	Flexible
Settled	Pending
Punctual	Leisurely
Purposeful	Responsive
Controls events	Adapts to events
Definite	Tentative
Product	Process

Now record your selected letters (E or I, S or N, T or F, J or P) in these blanks: _____, _____, _____, _____. The four letters you chose make up your four-letter type. If you chose the left-hand column exclusively, your four-letter type will be ESTJ. If you chose the right-hand column exclusively, your type will be INFP. These are called four-letter opposites. If your type is ESFP, then your opposite type is INTJ, and so on.

The Cognitive Functions

The cognitive functions are the two middle letters in your type. Your writing style is probably influenced more by the cognitive functions than by the attitudes (E and I) or the orientations (J and P). Remember that the first of the two middle letters (either S or N) is the perceiving function, and the second (either T or F) is the judging function. One of these two letters is the most preferred (or dominant) function, and the other is the second most preferred (or auxiliary) function.

It is particularly useful to know your dominant function since that's the one that will influence your writing style the most. For example, if your dominant function is S (sensing), you will probably like to write about your experiences using examples and concrete detail. If your auxiliary function is F (feeling), you will probably like to use a personal approach in writing about your experiences.

How to Find Your Dominant Function

1. Look at the last letter of your 4-letter type. It will be either J (judging) or P (perceiving). J or P points to which function you prefer to use in the outer world.
2. If J is your last letter, you show to the outer world the judging function, which is either thinking or feeling (T or F).
3. If P is your last letter, you show to the outer world the perceiving function, which is either sensing or intuition (S or N).
4. An extravert (E) will prefer to use the dominant function in the outer world. So for an extravert, the J or P points to the dominant function. Example: For an ESTJ, the dominant function is T.
5. An introvert (I) will prefer to use the dominant function in his or her inner world and to use the auxiliary in the outer world. So for an introvert, the J or P will point to the auxiliary function. The adjacent function will be the dominant. Example: For an INFP, the dominant function is F.

To illustrate, let's return to the ENFP student struggling to please her ISTJ professor. Remember that the "P" in her type points to the perceiving function (N), which she prefers to use in the outer world. Because she is an extravert, N is also her dominant function. The adjoining middle letter is F; that letter is her auxiliary, the function that "helps" her intuition. Her cognitive functions are NF.

Now let's consider her professor, the ISTJ. The J at the end of his type points to the judging function (T), which means that thinking is what he likes to use in the outside world. But thinking isn't his dominant function because an introvert uses the dominant in the inner world. Sensing is his dominant function, and thinking is his auxiliary function. His cognitive functions are ST.

Now find your own cognitive functions by going through the step-by-step process outlined above.

The Loomis-Grandstaff Writing Inventory

By the time we've reached adulthood, most of us have forgotten how to write our natural way. We're so used to being guided by teachers, supervisors, or writing books that we've lost touch with how we prefer to write. That's how writer's block happens. The Writing Inventory is designed to help you get back in touch with your preferred writing process.

In each pair, circle the letter of the statement that more accurately describes how you prefer to write. If you're unsure, choose the one that seems closer to your natural way of writing.

When you write, do you typically:

1. a. Plunge in and write quickly.
    b. Spend much of your time reflecting.
2. a. Talk to others about your ideas as you go along.
    b. Prefer to complete the writing project alone.
3. a. Generate many ideas and generalize about them.
    b. Write in depth about one or two ideas.

4. a. Discover your message as you go along.
   b. Figure out your message before you write.
5. a. Choose topics related to your outer world.
   b. Choose topics related to your inner experience.
6. a. Prefer to use an established pattern or format.
   b. Prefer to design your own format.
7. a. Focus on details and examples.
   b. Focus on meaning, possibilities, and the big picture.
8. a. Focus on individual sections of the paper.
   b. Focus on how the sections fit together.
9. a. Need clear directions for an assignment.
   b. Work easily with general guidance.
10. a. Present facts in a sequential or contextual order.
    b. Fit facts into a conceptual scheme.
11. a. Prefer to take a rational approach.
    b. Prefer to take a more personal approach.
12. a. Make and follow an outline to organize.
    b. Follow the flow of your thoughts to discover.
13. a. Make your point without considering audience response.
    b. Consider your audience's reaction.
14. a. Rely on reason and logical appeals.
    b. Rely on personal values and emotions.
15. a. Analyze the information objectively.
    b. Evaluate the information subjectively.
16. a. Decide on your topic quickly.
    b. Keep topic options open.
17. a. Choose narrow topics.
    b. Choose broad topics.
18. a. Gather necessary information quickly.
    b. Gather as much information as possible.
19. a. Finish your work ahead of time.
    b. Work up to the last minute.
20. a. Cut all but the necessities as you revise.
    b. Include as much information as you can.

To score the Writing Inventory, divide it into four groups of five. The first five items deal with extraversion and introversion. The (a.) answers involve using extraversion, and the (b.) answers involve using introversion. If you have a majority of (a.) answers, write down E. If you have a majority of (b.) answers, write down I.

Items six through ten deal with sensing and intuition. The (a.) answers involve using sensing, and the (b.) answers involve using intuition. If you have a majority of (a.) answers, write down S. If you have a majority of (b.) answers, write down N.

Items eleven through fifteen deal with thinking and feeling. The (a.) answers involve using thinking, and the (b.) answers involve using feeling. If you have a majority of (a.) answers, write down T. If you have a majority of (b.) answers, write down F.

Items sixteen through twenty deal with judging and perceiving. The (a.) answers involve using judging, and the (b.) answers involve using perceiving. If you have a majority of (a.) answers, write down J. If you have a majority of (b.) answers, write down P. Now record your four letters here:

_____ _____ _____ _____.

Compare these four letters to your four-letter personality type. Are they the same? At least the two letters in the middle (the cognitive functions) should agree.

Since writing is basically an introverted activity, more people score I than E on the Inventory. If you are an extravert but scored I on the Inventory, look at the way you start to write. Do you prefer talking with people before you start drafting and revising? Do you have trouble sitting down in isolation to reflect? Do you often learn what you want to say by talking it out with another person? Do you need to show your writing to others for feedback? Do you want to share what you have written very soon after you have written it? If you have answered "yes" to these questions, adjust your first letter on the Inventory to E.

Also, if your dominant function is either S or N and you are an introvert, consider how you answered the questions on the Writing Inventory relating to J and P (questions 16-20). Since writing is basically an introverted activity, you may have answered from your dominant perceiving function, which you introvert. Therefore, it may be more common for ISTJs, ISFJs, INTJs, and INFJs to score P on the Inventory.

Recognizing how you prefer to write is important. Otherwise, you will find yourself writing in a strained way and wasting much energy. Just as the MBTI helps you get in touch with your "true self" so that you don't waste energy trying to be someone you are not, the Inventory can help you get in touch with your true writing process.

Type and the Brain

The other day as I was looking for a belated birthday card, I came across one that read something like this: "My left brain is analytical, sequential, and orderly. My right brain is holistic, imaginative, and rhythmical. But it's that wide gap in the middle that caused me to forget my friend's birthday."

Actually, wide gaps and conflicting information abound in studies about the brain hemispheres. It's probably best, then, to start where most researchers agree. Most researchers generally believe that the two hemispheres have these distinct characteristics.

LEFT BRAIN	**RIGHT BRAIN**
One-at-a-time processing	All-at-once processing
Linear and systematic	Random and simultaneous
Focuses on details	Looks at the whole
Sees differences	Sees similarities
Receives verifiable information	Receives patterns
Is verbal	Uses images
Likes to distinguish and sort	Charts nuances
Analytical	Emotional
Likes definitions	Likes alliteration

Walter Lowen, an engineering professor and Jungian analyst, believes that the left and right brain hemispheres are most clearly linked to the orientations of judging and perceiving (16: pp. 7-8). Here's how he explains his theory:

Judging types favor the left hemisphere as they gather data; they generally focus on one thing at a time and "see one part of the field in an exact way." (The "field" refers to what we see as we look over our environment.) Perceiving types tend to prefer the right hemisphere as they gather data; that is, they can broadly process many things simultaneously and "see the entire field in an inexact way" (16: pp. 7-8).

Lowen further believes that the attitudes of extraversion and introversion are linked to the front and back of the brain. The front of the brain is responsible for acting on internal needs, such as hunger or discomfort, and it translates that need into a goal to do something about it. Lowen hypothesizes, then, that the characteristics which we call extraversion come from the front of the brain (16: p. 9).

The back of the brain is responsible for processing input from the external world. While the front brain says "act," the back brain says "reflect." Therefore, the characteristics we call introversion come from the back of the brain (16: p. 9).

In writing this workbook, I chose Lowen's study on brain activity because it has important implications for the writing process. For example, ENFPs have many ideas going on at once (right brain) and feel compelled to act on them (front brain). Because they also prefer intuition and feeling, ENFPs may be the most right-brain of all the types. (Another look at the right-brain characteristics will help clarify this idea.) ENFPs, then, will probably prefer to write about possibilities and how these possibilities affect the people they care about.

On the other hand, ISTJs prefer to focus on one idea at a time (left brain) and to reflect before they act (back brain). Because they also prefer sensing and thinking, ISTJs may be the most left-brain of all the types. (Look at the chart under left-brain characteristics.) ISTJs are more grounded in "what is" (or "was") than interested in "what could be" and will probably prefer to write impersonal reports or historical accounts.

According to Lowen, each type prefers to "gather data" uniquely according to brain function. For example, ENFPs prefer to gather data called "harmonies." ISTJs prefer to gather data called "sortings" (15: pp. 1-3).

Chapter Two, "The Writing Profiles," will show you how the ability to gather different kinds of data affects each type's writing style. But before you turn to Chapter Two, try some of these exercises to help you with the ideas presented in Chapter One.

Exercises:

1. Reflect on your early experiences as a student writer. Did you have an experience similar to the ENFP student in this chapter? If so, write a letter to the teacher who instructed you to write in his or her style. (Don't mail it!) If not, write a thank you letter to the teacher who encouraged you to write in your own style. (Do mail it!)

2. Reflect on what causes writer's block for you. Can you see a pattern that has caused anxiety? Write about this issue, perhaps in a journal.

3. If you could write about anything you wanted to in any way, what would it feel like? What kinds of writing do you like? Choose any topic and write it just the way you would like to.

4. Consider your attitude (E or I). Do you prefer to act before reflecting or reflect before acting? Do you like to talk over your project with a friend or colleague, or would you rather work alone? How does this preference affect the way you start to write?

5. Consider your orientation (J or P). Do you generally come to closure quickly about your topic, or do you generally spend much of your time gathering information? Write about how this preference affects your writing process.

Chapter Two:
The Writing Profiles

In Chapter One, you have most of the information you need to figure out your type. You've selected the four letters that make up your preferences, and you know your cognitive functions. The profiles in this chapter can help you confirm your type if you are mostly sure what it is, or they can help you to figure out your type if you are still somewhat unsure.

In the profiles, you'll find a general description of your personality type. This general description is based in part on Walter Lowen's research on how each type prefers to gather data (15: 1-3). Then you'll find a description of the writing style most likely to be "natural" for someone with your particular combination of preferences. The writing style descriptions draw on the profiles in *Writing and Personality*, by DiTiberio and Jensen (5: 66-124).

It may also be helpful to know that writers who prefer introversion (I) and intuition (N) are statistically in the minority. Therefore, if your type begins with these two letters (IN), your type is outnumbered. Keep in mind that your natural style is simply "uncommon" (statistically), not "wrong."

In order for you to find your profile quickly, I've grouped them according to the cognitive functions: Sensing Feeling (SF), Sensing Thinking (ST), Intuitive Feeling (NF), and Intuitive Thinking (NT). The phrase "feeling type" refers to people who prefer the feeling function; "thinking type" refers to those who prefer the thinking function; "sensing type" refers to those who prefer the sensing function; and "intuitive type" refers to those who prefer the intuitive function.

How to Read the Profiles

Find the profile for your four-letter type. Read over the general description to see if it describes the way you prefer to approach life and gather information. If the general description fits, read the writing style description. If this part also fits, then you can probably verify that this is your "true type," or at least your "best fit type."

If some of the parts fit, but other parts do not, then consider that one (or more) of your letters needs adjustment. Look particularly at letters that you may have conflict about. If you are a male and chose the thinking preference, it may be because it is culturally more acceptable for males to be thinking types. Consider looking at a feeling type profile. For example, if you came out ENTP and the profile doesn't quite fit, look at the ENFP profile to see if it is more like you.

Similarly, if you are a female and chose the feeling preference, it may be because it is more culturally acceptable for females to be feeling types. Consider looking at a thinking type profile. For example, if you came out ESFJ and the profile doesn't quite fit, look at the ESTJ profile.

If gender is not the issue, and neither profile seems to describe you very well, try some others until you find a description that works for you.

As you look at the dynamic pattern at the top of your profile, notice the order of the functions. The first is your dominant, the second is your auxiliary, the third is your tertiary, and the fourth is your inferior. Notice also the small e or i next to each cognitive function. These stand for extraversion and introversion, which, as you may remember, are called "attitudes." The cognitive functions operate differently according to the attitude they are in.

I'll discuss your dynamic pattern in more detail in Chapter Twelve. For now, simply note which attitude your first and second functions are in.

This chapter is mainly a resource for you to gain further insight into your type. If you work closely with other writers, you may want to read some of the other profiles. Observing the behavior of other writers and checking it by the profiles can help you understand their writing process – and understanding usually leads to a better work environment.

ESFJ:
Extraversion, Sensing, Feeling, Judging

Cognitive Functions:	***SF***
Dynamic Pattern:	***Fe***
	Si
	Ne
	Ti

General Description

ESFJs prefer to focus their energy on outer events and people and are probably the most sociable of all types. They show their feelings freely and like to experience warmth and harmony in their environment. Their sensing preference leads them to seek order and perform tasks in a sequential manner. Because they also have a preference for judging, they usually perform these tasks on schedule and can focus on them without feeling distracted. They love to coordinate, collaborate, organize, and see tangible results of their efforts.

This focus on order and organization leads ESFJs to be best at gathering data called "controls." To understand "controls," think of a machine or a computer and the amount of input it can handle. With certain input, it will produce a certain output. To translate this ability into type, ESFJs will do much planning to control the outcome of a situation, relying on past experience for information on how to deal with the present. They tend to collect and remember information that connects with people.

Writing Style

ESFJs write best about the personal – whether it is about people or personal experience. Enjoying collaboration in all things, they prefer to talk about their writing before getting it down on paper. They have a good sense of audience and work hard to please them. Indeed, of all the types, ESFJs are the most sensitive to indifference and need a solid relationship from a mentor, teacher, or editor. Because they wear their feelings on their sleeves, they may write prose that seems flowery or sentimental; in reality, it is a style that reflects the ESFJ's belief that "what is not felt cannot be thought."

For this reason, they will not enjoy writing about dry, dispassionate material. If they have to write this way, they may depend too heavily on "experts," citing them to prove a point they may feel neutral about. In their drive to please an authority figure, such as a boss or a teacher, they will usually learn how to write about technical topics or how to work modern technology. At the same time, they may not be good at remembering technical data that does not connect with people. They prefer writing narratives based on real-life situations. Whatever the topic, though, they like to stay on top of their projects and come to closure quickly.

ISFJ:
Introversion, Sensing, Feeling, Judging

Cognitive Functions: **SF**
Dynamic Pattern: **Si**
  Fe
  Ti
  Ne

General Description

ISFJs prefer to focus their energy inward as they gather data about their internal sensory impressions. This tendency to reflect on data from their senses leads them to enjoy history, facts, and other concrete information. They usually share their feelings (at least their positive feelings) about other people, preferring to live in harmony with them and to avoid conflict. Their preference for judging gives them the ability to focus well on their tasks and to stay in jobs that require routine, structure, and a schedule.

ISFJs generally store concrete data that the feeling function evaluates as worth knowing. They like and need clarity, and for that reason are the best type at gathering the data called "contrasts." "Contrasts" involve information that can be understood as clearly opposite. ISFJs can usually see the "do's" and "don'ts" of a situation and have an innate sense of what is appropriate. They don't usually act on impulse and like to reflect on clear-cut issues of "good or bad." They are generally dependable and loyal, practical and persistent. ISFJs seem to lend warmth and stability to whatever situation they are in.

Writing Style

ISFJs are likely to spend much time thinking about what they're going to write and how they're going to say it. Therefore, they may be "one-draft" writers, since much of the writing – and the revision – has already gone on in their heads. They like to write about personal experience, but may not want to share information that reveals their own psychology. In storytelling, they can be disarmingly funny since they have a knack for observing the quirks of humanity and capturing just the right quote or description to relay these quirks. They like to read historical fiction and may use it as a model for their own narratives.

ISFJs are one of the least likely types to enjoy technical or business writing. If they have to write this way, they may need a pre-existing format or model to guide them, such as a five-paragraph theme or an example that has worked before. They may resist modern technology, even when the job requires it or when it makes their job easier. Seeking clarity and shunning the ambiguous, ISFJs like to write easy-to-follow and well-ordered prose that reflects their sensitive and caring natures.

ESFP:
Extraversion, Sensing, Feeling, Perceiving

Cognitive Functions: **SF**
Dynamic Pattern: **Se**
   Fi
   Te
   Ni

General Description

ESFPs prefer to focus on the outer world of events and people and to take in as much information as they can through their senses. This preference for extraverted sensing often manifests in a love for the physical – sports, hiking, or dancing. They like to connect with people during social events, sharing jokes, stories, and games, but they dislike conflict. Since ESFPs prefer the perceiving orientation, they have an overall, rather than a focused, sense of their surroundings: they tend to know where everybody is sitting at a meeting, for example, but may not notice the color of the carpet. If their sense of hearing is well developed, they can remember who said what – and their tone.

This ability to take in their environment makes them good at gathering data called "matches." A "match" involves noticing similarities, especially those concerning people and their behavior. For this reason, ESFPs are usually accurate "type watchers." When in a conversation, ESFPs like to listen for what they can match to their own experience and then relate to it. This heightened awareness and sensitivity to whatever is going on around them makes ESFPs very much in tune with the here and now.

Writing Style

ESFPs can be good at writing about personal experience in the form of stories, anecdotes, or essays. They prefer to tell about their experience from a humorous perspective, or to tie it to the audience's experience. Since they are good at sizing up audiences, they can do this with relative ease. Part of relating to an audience and entertaining them is through using catchy phrases, puns, or quips. These come naturally to most ESFPs, and they are quick to share them. They are also good at dialogue and like to relay the spoken word through exclamation marks, capitalization, and underlining. ESFPs are performers, even on the page.

This focus on the spoken word gives their writing a clear sense of voice and vitality, but they have to be careful that more serious projects don't sound too anecdotal or conversational. They may not like to work with modern technology unless it is immediately useful or practical for their writing project. ESFPs usually need to share their ideas with a friend, supportive colleague, or writing group; then they can experience the "creative high" so vital to their success.

ISFP:
Introversion, Sensing, Feeling, Perceiving

Cognitive Functions: **SF**
Dynamic Pattern: **Fi**
                                    Se
                                    Ni
                                    Te

General Description

ISFPs prefer to focus their energy inward in order to reflect on their ideals, values, and internal harmony. Despite their introversion, they need contact with the world to connect with their sensing function, for it is through this function that they interact with their environment for concrete information. Their preference for the perceiving orientation keeps them flexible and adaptable as they take in a continuous stream of data about their physical world. Their feeling function evaluates this data, which they tend not to share except with special confidants or mentors. "Still waters run deep" may be the best way to describe this type.

Their emphasis on the natural world leads ISFPs to be best at gathering the data called "signals." "Signals" are sensory reactions: how it feels to look at red, to touch whiskers, to smell bread – or to miss a meal. Colors, tastes, sounds, smells, textures, comforts, and discomforts make more of an impression on ISFPs than on any other type; their world becomes real only through their physical experience of it.

Writing Style

ISFPs may find writing to be an intrusion because they are so private, with a particular reticence to share their "felt" experiences. The kind of writing they probably do best is description, especially if they have had a chance to handle the object they are describing. If they are describing a place, they will describe it more accurately if they can go there to experience the smells and colors. They may also need to do something physical, such as yoga or dancing, before they commit pen to paper. Writing about the natural world can be particularly inspirational to ISFPs – stories about plants, animals, or children, for example.

Because they are usually modest and eager to please, ISFPs need a solid relationship with those for whom they write. They will write more confidently if they have a model to work from. They may also need to check back with a mentor or boss for one-on-one feedback, as long as it's not too harsh. Even though ISFPs are at risk of losing their voice to others, with the right encouragement they can grace their prose with ample detail, descriptive colors, and keen perception.

ESTJ:
Extraversion, Sensing, Thinking, Judging

Cognitive Functions: **ST**
Dynamic Pattern: **Te**
                       Si
                       Ne
                       Fi

General Description

ESTJs prefer to focus their energy on the outer world of events and objects and to use this energy objectively and analytically. They like ordered tasks, step-by-step and sequential directions, practical plans, and lists. They are good at imposing deadlines on themselves, and if others impose the deadlines, they can easily schedule their time to meet them. Punctual and efficient, dutiful and responsible, they can organize their tasks and their environment. Their preference for sensing and judging helps them to focus on one thing at a time and to finish what they've started. Excellent at follow-through, they expect the same of others and usually get it because of their ability to manage workers. Based on the title, *The One-Minute Manager* would probably appeal to an ESTJ.

Because of their need for structure and output, ESTJs are best at gathering the data called "routines." "Routines" are tried and true sequences for how to produce a product or a result. ESTJs seem to have a sense of certainty that comes from knowing the sure way to get things done, which gives them an air of authority. For this reason, they are often asked to serve on boards or to take some other kind of responsibility in an organization. Others rely on their inherent "know-how."

Writing Style

ESTJs are best at writing documents based on standard operating procedure – guidelines, manuals, and sets of instructions. They may also excel at writing case studies because they have a need to make theoretical ideas concrete through documented real-life examples. If in careers that require routine correspondence, such as secretarial or administrative work, they may excel at writing business letters, memos, and reports. They have a knack for "putting the bottom line up top," or writing the main point first and then following it with supporting data. Adept at staying with a plan, they can handle details and accepted formats with ease.

ESTJs will probably not like to write about personal topics or their feelings – but may be good at writing clear, succinct descriptions. For this reason, they usually feel comfortable writing objective evaluations of an employee's performance or "Standard Behavioral Objectives." They may also be good at writing on controversial topics that allow them to take a stand.

ISTJ:
Introversion, Sensing, Thinking, Judging

Cognitive Functions: *ST*
Dynamic Pattern: *Si*
                              Te
                              Fi
                              Ne

General Description

ISTJs prefer to focus their energy inward as they take in concrete data such as smells, tastes, sounds, and other specific details about their environment. What they like to do with these details is to analyze them and put them into categories. They tend to be highly efficient and focused, with a preference for order and sequence. This type tends to be life's statisticians, librarians, bankers, and bookkeepers. They gravitate toward software that creates spreadsheets (such as Quicken) because spreadsheets provide something visual and sequential for dealing with finances. They like information that presents the "bottom line."

This focus on the quantifiable leads ISTJs to be the best at gathering data called "sortings." "Sortings" are those objects that can be ordered according to some objective and contrasting criterion such as size, amount, weight, color, or function. After ISTJs have sorted, then they are likely to make schedules to deal with the material they've sorted; thus they are highly capable of organizing not only themselves, but also corporations and companies. Because they are usually stable, reliable, and responsible, you can "take their word to the bank."

Writing Style

ISTJs are the most likely to enjoy writing the minutes of a meeting or reports about objective data. They may not like to write about people, but they can actually be quite good at characterization because of their ability to put people into categories of predictable behavior. Their introverted sensing helps them to be good at description since they can enliven a scene or object with ample detail and precise recall. Since they can picture the environment vividly, they can bring the past into the present – such as smells from Mother's kitchen.

This tendency to visualize also leads ISTJs to include graphs, tables, and charts in their reports. They use these visuals to illustrate the most important points rather than to lead the reader through the prose. They tend to have a formulaic approach to writing reports, referring to what has been done before so that they can be sure they have done it right. Clear, precise, and to the point, ISTJs may be the most efficient of all the writers, rarely suffering from writer's block or over-revising, especially when writing on business or technical topics.

ESTP:
Extraversion, Sensing, Thinking, Perceiving

Cognitive Functions: **ST**
Dynamic Pattern: **Se**
                             Ti
                             Fe
                             Ni

General Description

ESTPs prefer to focus their energy on outer events and objects and to use this energy to gather information about the concrete, physical world. They usually analyze this data objectively, enjoying the challenge of solving practical problems. They can take in many details at once, juggling and moving them around to apply to a variety of situations. Restless with a need for action, ESTPs are excellent negotiators and troubleshooters – and of all the types can best use their skills to turn a situation around. They have a high need to act on their environment.

ESTPs are good at gathering the data called "features." "Features" are the essential clues, or the bare outlines, needed to identify what is there. ESTPs tend to see what doesn't fit or what's important by noticing such details as facial expressions, slight movements, or crucial pauses. They may not tune into another person to empathize as much as to note how that person will react. "The Gambler" and "The Gunslinger" are roles fitting the ESTP's sense of timing and quick "take" of the environment.

Writing Style

ESTPs are most comfortable writing down details of their physical world so that in the end they can assemble them to see which ones they need. When describing an object or person, they need to look at these details, or clues, before they can feel confident about writing a coherent piece. Indeed, their first drafts may be filled with an overwhelming number of details and facts. ESTPs may also like to include visual details, such as flow charts, graphs, and tables, to highlight important information.

Quotations are other visuals ESTPs like to use, often organizing their prose around quotes because they represent concrete data. They may also need a tried and true format to begin a writing assignment. Once they have something to go on, they are quite good at adapting their writing to what has been previously written. They are not likely to "reinvent the wheel" if a model works well, but if it doesn't, they can modify it a bit to make it better. ESTPs dislike long explanations and, once they have gathered all their information, can pinpoint what is really important in a piece of writing. They tend to avoid "flowery" language or sentimentality and like to write on topics that have immediate or practical application.

ISTP:
Introversion, Sensing, Thinking, Perceiving

Cognitive Functions: **ST**
Dynamic Pattern: **Ti**
                              Se
                              Ni
                              Fe

General Description

ISTPs prefer to focus their energy inward with few distractions from the outside world as they reflect on analytical and objective data. They are hands-on and physical, preferring facts to the abstract or theoretical. ISTPs spend much of their time collecting data. Observant and casual, they like to work at their own pace with sudden bursts of energy rather than follow a routine. Though good at reading their physical environment, they may not act on it right away; instead, they first try to find out what is going on beneath what they are taking in.

Having keen powers of observation, ISTPs are best at gathering the data called "signs." A "sign" comes from an intimate, experiential knowledge of how something works. ISTPs are usually good with machines and like to tinker with them to find out more about them. Reading directions will usually take a back seat to this tinkering since ISTPs learn by doing. For this type, their knowledge is in their fingers. They can be excellent computer troubleshooters, since they like diagnosing the problem, and may even excel at complex databases. They can also be adept at landscape photography since they have a broad, sweeping view of their environment and like to be outdoors.

Writing Style

If ISTPs are describing an object, they will probably need to take it apart to identify every part and what it does. They may even want to know the background of an object; for example, if they are describing a camera, they may want to know when it was invented and what particular need it met at the time. If they are faced with a longer topic – one they are interested in – they will thoroughly research it, gathering multiple facts. In fact, they may not know when to quit, and if inspired, they are likely to work at a marathon pace until finished.

ISTPs tend to have an ironic, satirical sense of humor with a quick wit. They may neglect to think about others' reactions to their writing and for this reason may offend their audience, especially if they become too argumentative or defiant. They may also dislike writing about anything personally disclosing. However, if they are given the opportunity to write about their interests and from their keen observations, ISTPs can produce pieces that are clear, consistent, and thorough.

ENFJ:
Extraversion, Intuition, Feeling, Judging

Cognitive Functions:	**NF**
Dynamic Pattern:	**Fe**
	Ni
	Se
	Ti

General Description

ENFJs prefer to focus their energy on outer events and people and to freely express their feelings about these events. They enjoy the conversation and companionship of others, but they especially like being around people they care about. They are good at coming up with innovative ideas and at helping people understand the underpinnings of these ideas. Their preference for the judging orientation helps them to see ideas clearly, to "wrap things up," and to mobilize resources to get things done. In many cases, ENFJs can be heard articulating concepts that are hard to understand.

This emphasis on language helps ENFJs to be best at gathering the data called "associations." "Associations" are words that call up memories, feelings, or understandings. ENFJs find this language in literary, psychological, and religious texts, but particularly in the conversations of others. They are often capable and popular group leaders, acting as catalysts for positive change.

Writing Style

Highly intuitive and able to project their concern for others, ENFJs write best about topics that affect their own and other people's lives. Since they tend to be gregarious, they need to keep in regular contact with people to become inspired, and when they do, they can be highly persuasive. Of all the types, ENFJs are the most likely to get people to do what they don't want to, just through their adept use of language. "The pen is mightier than the sword" was probably coined by an ENFJ military leader.

ENFJs generally like to read and to clip just the right word or idea from a magazine or newspaper. They will enjoy writing about values and causes, embellishing them with their keen insight and vivid imaginations. Their content may be anecdotal, packed with hyperbole and other figurative language, but their value system will be evident throughout. Just as they enjoy being team leaders, they will probably enjoy leading a writing project and will use much of their energy seeing it through to completion. Expressive and persistent, ENFJs are almost always gifted communicators, whether in writing, speaking, acting, selling, or leading a workshop.

INFJ:
Introversion, Intuition, Feeling, Judging

Cognitive Functions: **NF**
Dynamic Pattern: **Ni**
                             Fe
                             Ti
                             Se

General Description

INFJs prefer to focus their energy on their inner world as they reflect on their keen insights and visions. Their feelings are strong with a deep sense of personal values, and they strive to find meaning in those feelings. INFJs seek to focus their strong intuitive hunches and ideas to come up with flashes of powerful images. Indeed, of all the types, they are the ones most likely to have psychic experiences.

INFJs tend to have a strong inner value system and are good at gathering the data called "preferences." "Preferences" are value judgments that are compared to each other and placed on a scale. INFJs are interested in ordered feelings in a wide range of categories – and this order can change according to what is going on in their lives. For example, someone or something might appeal to them at a particular time but not another, depending on their hunch or "feel" for the person or situation. Therefore, INFJs can have trouble deciding on some of their type preferences, especially Extraversion/Introversion.

Writing Style

Just as INFJs are sensitive to their preferences for authors and writing styles, they are also sensitive to how others react to their writing. They may nurture their ideas long before they commit them to paper in their zeal to have their writing affect others' lives. They tend to like "what if" questions and to find the one big idea that contains the answer or discovery. Visionary and original, INFJs are often fine novelists, but they can also write profound nonfiction; for example, they may write a book or article about a parent with Alzheimer's and how this disease is affecting the rest of the family.

INFJs usually like to read, and reading books by their preferred authors gives them more information for writing. They are often disciplined and may mete out designated times in the day to write, no matter what else comes up. Of all the types, they are the most likely to be published authors, even though they may give themselves unrealistic deadlines. Though their style may be somewhat formal, it is seldom dry because of the deep reservoir of their ideas and feelings. In fact, they can be the most passionate of all writers when they believe strongly in their topic. Readers usually sense INFJs' fierce commitment to their topic, and this commitment lends credibility and integrity to their style.

ENFP:
Extraversion, Intuition, Feeling, Perceiving

Cognitive Functions: **NF**
Dynamic Pattern: **Ne**
                        Fi
                        Te
                        Si

General Description

ENFPs prefer to focus their energy on outer events and people, and they spend much of this energy thinking of possibilities, meaning, and ideas. They like to think about the people they care about and to come up with ways to make their lives better. Their preference for the perceiving orientation opens their minds to even more possibilities for themselves and their loved ones. ENFPs like to stay open-ended and flexible, constantly considering all the options that come up in life.

ENFPs tend to be imaginative and innovative, seeking to please, and are at their best gathering data called "harmonies." "Harmonies" are ideas that may not be similar, but they balance one another and fit together. ENFPs are always trying out new scenarios in their jobs, looking for new experiences for themselves and others, and taking risks. They often begin with a burst of energy unrivaled by any other type. Their optimism and genuine love for life usually make them attractive, flexible, and empathetic colleagues with an original approach to all their many projects.

Writing Style

Since ENFPs hear what is pleasing, they are often good at intonation and word choice. They can tell when something hangs together since they have a feel for overall impression. They prefer to write about topics that affect people, and they can easily put themselves in others' shoes. In fact, many ENFPs can symbolically fuse their sense of self with their subject matter. Creative and insightful, they are excellent at analyzing motives and getting to the unstated feelings behind superficial language. Since they enjoy variety, they usually develop skills that allow them to excel at both imaginative and business writing. Indeed, they may even enjoy combining the two; for example, designing a workshop for businesses called "Harmony in the Workplace."

Because they seem to be continuously inspired to try something new, ENFPs may make more starts than finishes. For this reason, they can feel constrained by a writing deadline or feel blocked when the subject is routine or mundane. But if their feelings and ideals are invested, ENFPs can be excellent journalists and essayists, conveying a sophisticated and coherent style. They like to think of their writing as a puzzle with all the parts contributing to a harmonious whole.

INFP:
Introversion, Intuition, Feeling, Perceiving

Cognitive Functions: NF
Dynamic Pattern: Fi
   Ne
   Si
   Te

General Description

INFPs prefer to focus their energy on their inner world and therefore may need a great deal of time by themselves to reflect or dream. This inner world is punctuated by a strong need for harmony with their personal values and the people around them. What the outside world sees, however, is intuition, which they extravert in the form of possibilities, imaginative projects, and ingenious approaches to whatever they are dealing with. Their preference for the perceiving orientation relates to their ability to handle many ideas and projects at once. INFPs are often idealists, or even mystics, who need to find meaning in their lives – and can often help others do the same.

This emphasis on integrating the inner world with the outer world helps INFPs to be good at gathering data called "combinations." Working with combinations means putting entities together in a unique way. For example, INFPs are naturally adept at putting together sounds and words, as in rhymes and puns, and coming up with clever names or slogans. This ability to find combinations in language and ideas is often the key to their creativity.

Writing Style

INFPs are imaginative writers who gravitate toward poetry, metaphorical and alliterative language, and passionately persuasive prose. Because they are drawn to images, their descriptions may be quite vivid, not so much in the form of sensory detail but in scenes that capture the ambiance of an experience or a situation. Their thought pattern may meander like a stream or a stroll in the woods rather than follow a clear linear sequence, and for this reason their prose may ramble or reflect an elastic sense of time. But rarely is this prose mundane. INFPs at their best can produce writing that combines a strong sense of the aesthetic, a keen insight, and a concern for higher values.

INFPs can write well on scientific subjects if they are inspired. Perhaps it was an INFP neurobiologist who wrote about how the combination of receptors in the nose helps us to distinguish smells. However, INFPs will probably dislike writing anything that smacks of the bureaucratic. When asked to write Standard Behavioral Objectives (SBOs) for her students, an INFP teacher refused. Instead, she wrote a page filled with her feelings about writing SBOs, and she was excused from the project.

ENTJ:
Extraversion, Intuition, Thinking, Judging

Cognitive Functions: **NT**
Dynamic Pattern: **Te**
                              Ni
                              Se
                              Fi

General Description

ENTJs prefer to focus their energy on the outer world of events and objects. They are big picture people as they gather information about their abstract, intuitive world. They like to come to closure quickly and work with a plan. ENTJs are life's natural leaders – they know how to take charge and seem to be born to organize groups. Though they enjoy working with other people, they may prefer to act on their own conclusions rather than on someone else's.

ENTJs place great emphasis on the whole tied together by invisible connections, which leads them to be the best at gathering data called "structures." A "structure" is the form beneath a complex system, such as the anatomy of the human body or the Human Genome Project in the field of genetics. It is the simplest way of holding the largest amount of information together so that there is order underneath the chaos. They like to put concepts together piece by piece or take them apart the same way to come up with the underpinnings of a network or pattern. As counselors, they can be good at working with family structures, and as educators, they can excel at designing the structure of a class or text.

Writing Style

ENTJs look for intellectual clarity in their own and others' writing. They like to have a plan before they begin so that they can see where the parts might be heading. So strong is their need for competence that they might place unreasonable demands on themselves and others in their drive for mastery and achievement. Given all of this, then, it is better for everyone if they are allowed to take the lead in a writing project. They often make good mentors to other writers since they can help them solve their writing problems step-by-step to come to a coherent whole.

Because they focus so much on the message – and the efficiency of that message – they sometimes ignore connection to audience. Therefore, they may need an early realistic appraisal of their writing from someone they respect, such as an editor who can show them where to put in personal examples, how to tone down what may be an abrasive tone, and how to add more warmth. When ENTJs receive this feedback, they are perhaps the most competent of all the types at writing about complex, abstract theory that serves a valuable and useful purpose.

INTJ:
Introversion, Intuition, Thinking, Judging

Cognitive Functions: **NT**
Dynamic Pattern: **Ni**
                                     Te
                                     Fi
                                     Se

General Description

INTJs prefer to focus their energy on their inner world as they reflect on designs, concepts, and "inner knowings." They are naturally adept at cause and effect, analysis, and problem solving. The combination of their thinking and intuition preferences makes for a type drawn to models and systems, and INTJs are usually quite competent in producing these. They can see what needs to be done and get the job done quickly.

Given this ability for objectivity and analysis, INTJs are best at gathering data called "logic." "Logic" deals with defining relationships by some system of rules or theory. Indeed, INTJs may not accept anything that doesn't make sense, isn't rational, or doesn't include facts that lead to a logical conclusion. Pragmatic and methodical, INTJs are eager to put their theories to practical use.

Writing Style

INTJs' style is usually business-like and concise, and therefore may not be as developed as it could be. Driven as they are to conclusions, they may have the conclusion in mind even as they start to write the introduction. In fact, all of their efforts work forward to find the conclusion or backward to prove it. For this reason, their prose may have an ultimate quality to it, as though they have found the one and only answer. INTJs are good at writing reports that need to provide answers or show results. They may also like to define unfamiliar terms since they have a natural propensity for clarifying the ambiguous.

INTJs like to think about big picture ideas. If they are scientists, they may like to read science fiction or to ponder the likelihood of the sun burning up in five billion years. If they are theologians, they may write about their conversations with God so as to clear up the mystery. Because they are so good at grasping big concepts, INTJs excel at working with large projects. They prefer to see the project as a "dynamic system" with facts and theory intertwined instead of as separate entities. To them, sensing is not separate from intuition, but rather sensing is a necessary counterpart to intuition. Their projects are often full of visuals to provide a logical progression through the prose. Most readers appreciate the clarity and organization that INTJs bring to their writing and the confidence that exudes from their style.

ENTP:
Extraversion, Intuition, Thinking, Perceiving

Cognitive Functions: **NT**
Dynamic Pattern: **Ne**
 Ti
 Fe
 Si

General Description

ENTPs prefer to focus their energy outward on events and objects as they explore new possibilities and "paradigm shifts." They are usually good at critical analysis and can find the flaw in arguments. Their preference for the perceiving orientation, coupled with their preference for intuition, prompts them to generate options for just about any situation, as they love to be challenged and to challenge others. They tend to be entertaining presenters, excellent debaters, and insightful visionaries as they seek external stimulation and look for the big picture.

This ability to generate options and stimulate their environment helps ENTPs to be the best at gathering data called "patterns." A "pattern" is a common thread that runs through entities or elements to hold them together. ENTPs are very skillful at handling large amounts of information and can accept or reject it according to the pattern they hold in their heads. This pattern may be like a gigantic web (like the Internet) that gives ENTPs a sense of order even in the midst of chaos. The Enneagram may appeal to ENTPs because it points to patterns of behavior.

Writing Style

ENTPs are often clever idea people who like to create an intellectual scheme. For this reason, they may enjoy designing writing programs or seminars more than going through the tedious details of producing a document. But when they do produce, the result is usually quite thorough because of their propensity to gather incredibly complex information and present it coherently. ENTPs are stimulated by problem-solving or controversial topics, and if asked to defend their views or visions, they can usually "best" their challenger.

ENTPs often have a playful sense of humor and can be witty at someone else's expense. In fact, they often like to test the limits of authority just to see if they can "get away with it." If they don't, they are unlikely to feel remorse because taking the risk is worth the result, even when the result goes against them. For this reason, they can be quite good at political satire and comedy writing. They may not like traditional methods of composition and usually try to find an original way to write even the most mundane pieces of communication. But if ENTPs are allowed to write their own way, they can make complex conceptual models clear, concise, and interesting, even to lay readers.

INTP:
Introversion, Intuition, Thinking, Perceiving

Cognitive Functions: NT
Dynamic Pattern: Ti
Ne
Si
Fe

General Description

INTPs prefer to focus their energy inward and to use their imaginations to reflect on ways to understand and categorize. They tend to enjoy the theoretical and abstract. They like to think about rational approaches to the data they collect and to find order even in complex material. They can handle a variety of subjects and projects at once and come up with inventive options for dealing with them. Having an intense curiosity and a high need to analyze a task, they can become consumed with a project for hours. Of all the types, INTPs most love the challenge of solving problems and doing the seemingly impossible.

Because they are so adept at coming up with solutions, INTPs are the best at gathering data called "strategies." A "strategy" is a plan for carrying out a complex task, but it is not a straight-forward plan. A strategy in this sense involves surprising twists and turns and may even be the longest distance between two points. Their strategy often results in projects with an aesthetic flow or in an improvement to the status quo. Even though their main interest is in solving problems, INTPs will still want to thoroughly understand the underpinnings or root of the problem before acting on it.

Writing Style

INTPs do their best work alone; they are highly independent and will tend to shun anything formulaic. They prefer writing about theoretical subjects – such as physics, psychology, or religion – and are quite adept at seeing the connections among these subjects. In writing about physics, their imagination may trigger a similar idea in psychology and then in religion. INTPs will quickly see the underlying "law" connecting these three; for example, quantum physics as it relates to Jung's collective unconscious as it relates to the Chinese concept of "The Tao."

If INTPs cannot find a theory for their insights, they may make one up and support it with much rationale. They are excellent at clarifying dense material and often include definitions for their abstract words and analogies for their concepts. Even so, readers may need a dictionary when reading INTPs' prose because of their extensive vocabulary. Incisive and insightful, they can get to the essence of the subject even as they use metaphorical language. Drawn to academia, INTPs are quintessential professors and researchers, heavily invested in their material.

Questions to Consider:

1. What is accurate about your profile? What is not accurate? What would you add to or subtract from your profile? If your profile does not ring true, read through the profiles until you find the one most like you. You might then want to adjust a letter or two in your four-letter type.

2. Look at the two middle letters of your four-letter type (the cognitive functions). Based on what you know about these letters, what kind of writing assignments would feel most natural for you?

3. Look up another profile that has the same cognitive functions but different attitudes or orientations. How is this type most like you? How is it different?

4. Look up your four-letter opposite. (Example: The opposite of an ENFP is ISTJ.) How would you feel if you had to write like this personality type? What would you do to please this type if he or she were your teacher or supervisor?

5. Read over the profiles and find one that describes a writing teacher or supervisor you once had. Did this person insist that you write in his or her style? If so, how did this affect you as a writer?

The Four Stages of the Writing Process

Introduction

In this workbook, I compare the four stages of the writing process to the stages for building a house. Why a house?

In *House as a Mirror of Self*, Claire Cooper-Marcus writes about how our houses can be sacred space for the expanding sense of self. As an example, she notes Carl Jung's account of building his stone tower retreat on the lake at Bollingen in Switzerland. Jung built the tower in four stages as the "impulse to expand emerged in him." Jung believed that each addition to his tower expressed some new dimension of himself (2: p. xiv).

As you go through each stage of the writing process, you'll find that some new dimension of yourself will begin to emerge. In the first stage, you tap your imagination for ideas that may not yet be in your conscious awareness. In the second stage, you begin to organize your ideas into a form that feels natural for you. In the third stage, you develop your material by drawing on the unused parts of your personality to flesh out content and to address the needs of the audience. And in the fourth, you revise your writing to smooth out the rough edges.

Now compare this process to the stages of constructing a house. What is the first thing you would do? You would probably dream a lot, either in your head or on paper. You would gather many ideas and images – you would engage your imagination. Your dream house might range from a log cabin to a contemporary. In this first stage, you are a dreamer, so anything goes.

After you've decided what kind of house you would like to have, you're ready to make your dream a reality. You then make some kind of framework or plan so that you can envision the house. What kind of theme will predominate? How will the house be laid out? In this second stage, you are a designer who will draw the blueprint for the house.

Now that the house has taken shape, you're ready to flesh out your plan. What will give the house substance? How will the rooms look? Where will they be placed? Will everything fit together? Will it meet the needs of everyone who lives there? In this third stage, you are a builder who focuses on the "content" of the house.

Finally comes the detail work. Is the color scheme effective? Are the edges around the cornices smooth? Does the wiring work? Is the house comfortable, convenient, and tastefully done? In this fourth stage, you are an inspector with your eye on the finished product.

Keep in mind that comparing the writing process to building a house is figurative. To take the analogy literally would be like saying, "Oh, I hated building my house, so I may as well give up on the writing process too." However, I've found as a writing teacher that many people would rather build a house than write a paper. Perhaps the house analogy can help make the writing process seem more concrete and less vague.

Facing and Overcoming Resistances

Each personality type may have some resistances to the stages of the writing process as I describe them. Sensing thinking types (ST) may balk at the names "dreamer" and "designer." The word "dreamer" may not feel practical or grounded. Sensing thinking types may find it difficult to "get in the flow" of the unconscious mind to tap their creativity in the Dreamer Stage. The word "designer" may feel too much like a "big picture" skill to sensing thinking types because they usually see the parts before they see the whole.

Sensing feeling types (SF) may feel some resistance to the word "dreamer" because of the emphasis on using the imagination. Sensing feeling types are usually literal rather than imaginative, relying heavily on concrete experience. However, this type will usually be open to and conscientious about whatever the author or the teacher suggests. Sensing feeling types may feel intimidated by the word "designer" because of the idea of finding the one main idea out of all the details.

Intuitive thinking types (NT) may experience some resistance to the word "dreamer" because of the feeling tone associated with it. However, the word "designer" will probably appeal; indeed, this personality type is usually the architect and designer of buildings. The word "inspector" may sound too tedious to this type because they are more interested in the big picture and larger concepts than details.

Intuitive feeling types (NF) will probably be intrigued by the word "dreamer" because it engages their imagination. Also, the word "designer" will probably appeal because it suggests flexibility in moving parts around to fit the big picture. While "builder" is a word that appeals more to the other types, intuitive feeling types will likely enjoy the Builder Stage once they realize it involves learning new skills to improve their writing. Since the word "inspector" conjures up images of detail work, such as checking for typos and formatting correctly, intuitive feeling types may resist this word.

No word, skill, or technique is going to please all the types. Getting past resistances is one of the reasons for writing from your preferences. Once you give yourself permission to go with what feels natural, then it feels safer to venture into the parts that you are resisting.

So keep your mind open! In Chapter Three, "The Dreamer," you will learn some general techniques to tap your creative right brain to begin writing. Chapter Four suggests specific techniques for your personality type to try in the Dreamer Stage.

Chapter Three:

The Dreamer

What image does the word "creative" evoke for you? Do you think of a genius sitting alone as a light bulb flashes, yielding sudden insight? Perhaps you think of an artist at her easel painting a masterpiece, or a scientist in his lab discovering a cure for a dreaded disease. But the truth is that we are all creative; indeed, creativity is the main thing that separates us from lower forms of mammals.

We cannot foresee what our creativity will bring, but we can attempt to understand the force of human creativity. This is important because we now know that the future is closely tied to how we humans use our creativity. The result of how we use our creativity may be determined in large part by our dreams and the struggle to make them real. What we dream is eventually what we create; without a dream, we have nothing to go on and no incentive to create (3: p. 6).

Consider your dream house. The seed has been planted, and you start dreaming about the space you would like to live in. Maybe you yearn to get away from big-city life, and you see yourself in a farm house in New Hampshire. The ceilings have large beams, and the floors are hardwood. The windows look out on fields of wildflowers and old barns. Living in this house suits your need to turn inward and reflect.

Or perhaps you see yourself living in a townhouse where you can walk to markets, the theater, and museums. You envision yourself surrounded by plants and pottery and colorful, exotic rugs. The paintings on your walls are by Gauguin in Tahiti. Your townhouse has a spiral staircase leading up to a loft where you go to read a favorite mystery or to work on your writing. A staircase leads down to a recreation room where you entertain.

Most dreams start with some kind of yearning that comes up from the unconscious, whether it is a dream house or a piece of writing that seeks expression. The house or writing has to be dreamed into being. The writing may be as simple as a memo or as complex as a novel, but all successful writing starts out with an idea of what you want it to be, even if all you want it to be is clear communication.

The purpose of the Dreamer Stage is to generate and capture ideas and to let the imagination go free – to create. When our creativity is blocked, we start getting picky. We edit too much. In short, we allow our "inner critic" to emerge, and we judge our work too soon. To get into the Dreamer Stage, then, we have to get away from "shoulds and oughts" and preconceived notions of what's right or wrong, such as outlines or notecards. Since the inner critic, or our ego chatter, slows us down, we need to put it aside to allow the unconscious to emerge. Tapping the unconscious helps us to be more receptive, and then we become like a magnet to ideas.

In the Dreamer Stage, no idea is too foolish, no story irrelevant, no joke inappropriate. In effect, we play on paper. The word "play" comes from the Latin word "ludic," and in this stage we allow ourselves to be ludicrous or playful.

Whimsical, creative, playful – what other words come to mind when you think of a dreamer? Add your words under the Dreamer columns on the next page.

Dreamer			
whimsical	creative	playful	imaginative
child-like	full of wonder	chaotic	free

Techniques for the Dreamer Stage

Think of the techniques as tools you can rely on for the rest of your life as a writer, not simply exercises for this chapter. If your inner critic starts to emerge as you go through the techniques, think of him as a squeaking mouse and close him up in a jar with a tight lid. Or imagine her as a grumpy cartoon character who has no power over you. Tell the critic that she will have a chance to help you revise your writing later, but right now, the dreamer is free to create.

Freewriting

Freewriting is writing freely without judging your content. One idea leads to another without logical coherence – the ideas flow into one another unfettered by the constraints of the ego. If a joke comes to mind, write it down. If you are suddenly reminded of an anecdote or story, write that too. Bits and pieces of conversation or dialogue may suddenly come into mind as you are describing a person – write those down. Because freewriting is so quick and flowing, you might be surprised by what comes from your pen. There is no quicker way to get over writer's block than to freewrite for ten minutes or so.

In *Writing with Power*, Peter Elbow talks about five benefits of freewriting (6: pp. 14-16).

1. Freewriting for ten minutes is a good way to warm up when we sit down to write something. We won't waste so much time getting started when we turn to our real writing task, and we won't have to struggle so hard to find words.

2. Freewriting helps us write when we don't feel like writing. It is practice in setting deadlines for ourselves and learning gradually how to get that special energy that sometimes comes when we work fast under pressure. It teaches us to write without thinking about writing – to just say it.

3. Freewriting is a useful outlet. We have a lot in our heads that makes it hard to think straight and write clearly: we are mad at someone, sad about something, perhaps even "inconveniently happy." Freewriting is a quick outlet for these feelings so that they don't get in our way.

4. Freewriting helps us to think of topics to write about. If we just keep writing, following threads where they lead, we will get to ideas, experiences, feelings, or people that are just asking to be written about.

5. Finally, freewriting improves our style. It leads to powerful writing because it taps the insight that comes from putting aside our conscious, controlling self. It helps us stand out of the way and let words be chosen. In this way, freewriting gradually puts a deeper voice into our writing.

What makes freewriting so freeing is that it comes spontaneously from the right side of the brain. The left side thinks logically. It conjures up "just the facts, Ma'am," as Jack Webb used to tell the befuddled woman on the TV show "Dragnet." If we let the left brain in too soon, it will surely warn us that our sentences are ending in prepositions and that a comma is out of place.

The right side is impulsive, random, and creative. It responds to images and ideas and rhythmical language. It has a sense of humor; it can be downright corny and may enjoy a good old practical joke. It loves surprise, and color, and wonder. It is what some psychologists call "your inner child," and this child may even want to have a tantrum on paper! (By the way, the right brain loves exclamation marks.)

Try it. In the space provided, write nonstop on a topic for about ten minutes. If you have to write a paper for a difficult teacher, address that teacher's demands. If you have to write a memo to a cranky boss, tell him how his crankiness is affecting the rest of the office. Tell him that he reminds you of a disapproving parent. Picture his scowl, and tell him that you don't like the new policy he's trying to push through – and why. Whatever your topic, write quickly and don't worry about mistakes. The purpose is to free up the creative energies of the right brain.

Freewrite

_____

_____

_____

_____

_____

_____

_____

_____

_____

_____

_____

_____

_____

_____

_____

_____

_____

_____

_____

_____

_____

_____

_____

When we freewrite, we use our pen as an expression of power. And when we arrive at that sudden piece of truth or make a discovery or express authentic feelings, we truly do feel free.

Clustering

Writers need some "magic key" for getting in touch with their imaginative power. In *Writing the Natural Way*, Gabriel Rico calls clustering that magic key because it gets past the logical left brain into the world of daydreaming, random thought, and imagination. It is the gate to the unknown. Wondering – or dreaming – is the natural state at the beginning of all creative acts. Clustering helps us to wonder (25).

To create a cluster, begin with a nucleus word, circled on a piece of paper. Then simply let go and begin to flow with any connections that come into your head. Write these down quickly, each with its own circle, connecting each new word or phrase with a line to the preceding circle. When something new strikes you, begin again at the central nucleus and radiate outward until you tap as many associations as you can in about five minutes.

Here's an example of a cluster from a student in my writing workshop. The assignment was to bring an object from work or home that had meaning. This student clustered a paperweight on her desk. From her cluster, she wrote an essay on how paperwork was taking over her life and weighing her down.

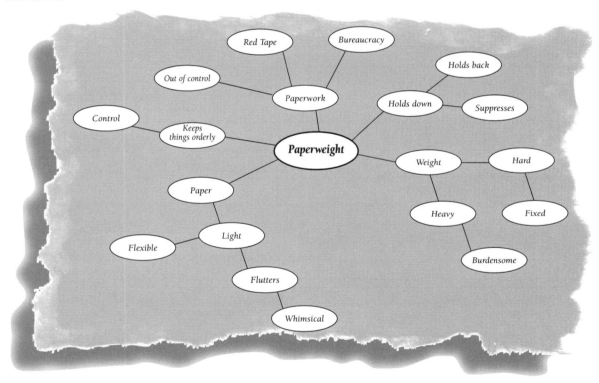

There's no right or wrong way to cluster. Simply begin to associate; the insights and connections will come. Clustering is more natural than outlining or listing because it works in a more random way, just as our minds do. It's playful and therefore reduces anxiety about writing. If you experience "clusterer's block," start doodling with the lines and arrows and circles to trigger an association.

I sometimes draw my clusters in an oval shape, like an egg. I think of the plastic eggs at Eastertime – those eggs that snap apart revealing a surprise inside. Inside each egg-like cluster is a surprising thought or image or connection coming up from the unconscious. Each piece of the cluster is like breaking open the "cosmic egg" that spawned creation. This is especially true in April as I watch the earth open up or come alive with freshness and new growth. The word "April" comes

Write from the Start

from the Latin "Aperio," which means "to open," as in "aperture"; clustering helps open up my imagination to give my writing freshness and new growth.

Try it. Write a word in a circle (or oval) in the middle of the open space provided. It can be a feeling word, such as "fear," or it can be the topic of the memo you've been putting off. It can be the name of that boss who is intimidating everybody in the office or a class that is a challenge for you. Perhaps it's a problem you've been trying to solve. When you cluster, don't worry about being neat and orderly. Just relax and wonder.

Cluster

Listing

Another technique for capturing ideas and gathering information is listing. Jot down a "grocery list" of images, words, phrases, or sentences that come to mind as you think about your topic. Let your mind flow freely. Jot down images and impressions wherever you are – in a restaurant, in an art museum, or at the airport. Listing, or jotting, helps you to be more observant and to notice details.

You might try listing according to the senses. Make five headings: Sight, Sound, Touch, Smell, and Taste. Then look around a room in your house (or dorm or apartment) and list anything that pertains to each sense. I chose my kitchen as an example because it's the room that usually taps all of the senses.

Sight	Sound	Touch	Smell	Taste
herbs	clatter	firm	roasted	sour
plants	sizzle	soft	burnt	sweet
oak cabinets	steam	sharp	fragrant	bitter
tiled floors	crunch	mushy	pungent	oily
orange	chop	wet	subtle	tart
blue	boil	rough	strong	salty

Try it. Look around your office or room or yard and notice what is there. Observe the shades of colors and notice patterns. Look closely at the pictures on your walls, or pick up an object and describe its shape, texture, and colors. List all details in the space below.

_____

_____

_____

_____

_____

_____

_____

_____

_____

_____

_____

_____

_____

_____

_____

_____

How was this experience for you? What nuances did you observe that otherwise would have escaped your attention? Did you become more absorbed with the scene or the picture or the object?

Write from the Start

Paying attention to an object or a person or a place is an act of connection. To what extent did you feel this sense of connection?

Active Imagination

Active imagination is a dialogue with the unconscious to integrate images that arise into consciousness. It is somewhat like our night-time dreaming in that we are relating to symbolic images, but we are awake. Because these images have a mind of their own, they say things that are surprising to us if we don't try to control their responses. Some people who regularly perform active imagination exercises find that their night dreams decrease because they are making the unconscious more conscious (12: pp. 137-221).

Active imagination dialogues help us to focus and to avoid getting lost in daydreaming, which so often leads to procrastination or even paralysis. You can write the dialogues on the computer, but writing them by hand is often more natural and connects you more directly to your creativity.

The first step in writing a dialogue with the images of the unconscious begins by taking your mind off the external world and focusing on the imagination. You invite the images to emerge, to communicate with you. If your mind goes blank, just wait until something comes up – a place, a person, an object, or an animal. The image may even be a negative emotion such as inferiority, especially if society has given you negative messages about your gender or race. These are not pleasant to face, so we often want to run away from them, but these are usually the very images we need to deal with.

Once you have found the image or the emotion you want to write about, the second step is to relinquish control. Let your imagination move freely so that you can daydream effectively. Let it go to a place, like a favorite vacation spot, so that you will feel more relaxed and apart from everyday stresses. If a mood is obsessing you, a dialogue with that mood is an effective way to stop repressing it so that it doesn't interfere with your work.

The third step is the dialogue itself. Remember that the key is to listen to the image rather than try to control its responses. You can begin by asking questions such as, "Why are you in my life?" or "What do you want from me?" Then the image (person, mood, place, animal) answers. Dialoguing with an animal or a part of nature can be particularly effective because these represent some instinctual part of ourselves. Here's an example of a dialogue with an animal (28: 121-122).

Me:	Owl, why do you hoot outside my window at night?
Owl:	Because I am the bird of the dark, the unseen.
Me:	Why are you visiting me?
Owl:	I have a message for you.
Me:	What is the message?
Owl:	I see that which others cannot. When you are deceived, I see and know what is really there.
Me:	Are you trying to tell me to look at deceptions?
Owl:	No one can deceive you about what they are doing. You see through people's ulterior motives.
Me:	What are you asking me to do?
Owl:	I am helping you to see the truth. I am asking you to use your powers of keen, silent observation to intuit some life situation.
Me:	How do I do this?
Owl:	Befriend the darkness inside yourself. Ask yourself what you are in the dark about.

Me: But I don't like the darkness, the unknown.

Owl: Don't be afraid. Soon, the bright light of dawn will illuminate you. Pay attention to your life. The truth always brings further enlightenment.

Me: Thank you, Owl. Do you have a final word for me?

Owl: Remember that I am always asking, "Who?"

Children, especially, can benefit from writing a dialogue with an animal. If you are an elementary teacher, I suggest that you encourage this technique since children are often closer to the natural world than adults are.

In *Ladder of Years*, Anne Tyler's heroine says that in learning to love, start with a rock, then a tree, and then a cloud before you "graduate" to loving a person. Perhaps in learning to write authentically, we can start by embracing the instinctual or natural parts of ourselves. Then we can "graduate" to the more complex interactions between ourselves and other people.

If you do write an active imagination dialogue with a real person, such as your boss, be sure to listen carefully to his or her responses, especially if you are angry. Through the responses, you may gain some insight into your boss's behavior, which may prevent you from acting out your anger in real life. It will also help you to be more tactful and understanding when you do write that memo.

Try it. Let an image come to you. If it is a real person in the external world, just ask questions without judging and without getting heavily invested in your emotions. This is a good exercise to follow a freewrite in which you have expressed your real feelings. In contrast to freewriting, active imagination dialogues help you to be more objective about your feelings. Instead of using the exercise to tell a person off, for example, use it to get more clarity about that person.

Active Imagination Dialogue

_____

_____

_____

_____

_____

_____

_____

_____

_____

_____

_____

_____

_____

_____

_____

You may find that some of the responses surprise you. Surprise responses usually occur about half way into the dialogue when the ego lets go of control.

The Dreamer Stage has much to do with getting down on paper that which you did not know that you knew. The first step is to get in touch with the unconscious mind to tap the resources that lie within. When the writing hand learns to flow freely with the imagination, then you can capture ideas that are just begging to be expressed.

Exercises to activate your imagination:

1. Think of a childhood memory. Begin with the phrase "I remember" and freewrite for 10 minutes.

2. Now take that same memory and cluster some associations. What new connections arise from the cluster that didn't occur in the freewrite?

3. Take an emotion, such as grief or joy, and write it in a circle in the middle of the page. Cluster as many associations that come to mind with this word.

4. Write a dialogue between yourself and someone who has been an important part of your life. This person may no longer be living. Try not to monitor or control the responses.

5. Find a picture in a magazine and jot down your impressions. Quickly list any details you see, including shape and color. Now cluster that picture for more associations.

6. Think of a course you're taking right now or one that you have recently taken. Write an active imagination dialogue with some part of that course or perhaps with the instructor. If it is a literature course, you might choose a character from a book or play. What insights have you gained about that course, instructor, or character?

7. Think of a challenging assignment or task and do a freewrite. If you still feel stuck after the freewrite, cluster that assignment or task.

8. Think of a turning point in your life. Imagine the events turning out another way. (For example, imagine that you did marry that old flame or go to that other school or take that other job.) Using any or all of the methods in this chapter, rewrite the turning point.

9. Dialogue with a room in the house where you grew up or a room in the house (or dorm) where you live now. How does this space speak to you?

10. Imagine that you are the opposite sex. Dialogue with yourself as the other gender.

Chapter Four:
Using Your Preferences in the Dreamer Stage

Now that you're familiar with some general ways to start gathering information, think about how you prefer to get started. Not all of the techniques will appeal to you. Some will feel more natural than others, or you may think of other ways that I haven't mentioned. Take outlining, for instance. Most of us were taught to outline as the way to start. Given that, let's look at outlining as a way to start writing.

By its nature, outlining is a structured, linear, left-brain process. It involves numbers, letters, order, sequence – the very opposite of the random way our brains work when ideas start flowing. Some people, depending on their type, will be tempted to put these ideas in outline form just as they are about to take a surprising turn or lead to an association or connection.

It is far better to freewrite, cluster, list, or dialogue than to outline in the Dreamer Stage. Outlining has its place, but it is not when you are freely gathering and capturing ideas. If you do decide to outline, call it a preliminary outline so that you can go back and expand on an idea when it comes. You are much more likely to experience writer's block when you structure the imagination prematurely. You want to "free" your creativity, not "freeze" it.

Writer's block is best described as the inability to make a decision at some point in the writing process. In short, it is the feeling of being hopelessly stuck and desperately wishing you were doing something else. However, when you start to write in a way that nurtures your innate personality, you can discover how to navigate writing roadblocks. This chapter points you in the right direction.

You will find your type grouped according to cognitive functions: SF, ST, NF, and NT. You will then find a guideline of what would appeal to your type in the Dreamer Stage, including your "tendencies" (your probable strengths) and "troublespots" (possible weaknesses). The "tools to try" should help you to move quickly out of that quagmire we all know as writer's block.

Sensing Feeling: SF

ESFJs:

Tendencies

- can usually sense how much time is needed for a project
- like to choose personal topics based on experience
- enjoy collaborative projects
- need to talk about their ideas
- accept direction easily and act on it quickly
- need a lot of input from a mentor, teacher, or boss
- have a solid sense of audience
- are comfortable with details and facts

Troublespots

- may resist clustering because of their need for order and efficiency

- may not like to write active imagination dialogues
- may resist including information deemed irrelevant in their eagerness to come to closure
- may dislike technical or dry topics
- may not function well in isolation
- may "boilerplate" too readily or rely on authorities' opinions

Tools to Try

- Put in the people, no matter what the topic.
- Write about your feelings and sentiments.
- Put a control on the Dreamer Stage by writing timed freewrites.
- Relate to the audience from the start.
- Talk to others, limiting time that you reflect.
- If stuck, do something active, such as having lunch with a friend or taking a walk.
- Generate as much detail as you can by listing.
- Write from a model if the topic is unfamiliar or technical.

ISFJs:

Tendencies

- need clear instructions for the writing project
- like to pause and reflect often during freewrites
- like to generate many facts, examples, and supporting data
- are good at using subtle wit
- can usually sense how much time is needed to gather material
- feel most comfortable using tried and true methods
- need privacy for this stage
- are good at creating from something already existing

Troublespots

- may not like trying new techniques, such as clustering
- may resist dreaming on the computer, even if it will save time
- may have trouble with more esoteric topics, such as psychology or philosophy
- may feel low energy dealing with technical topics
- may have trouble taking a stand on controversial topics
- may reflect too much before writing
- may revise a freewrite if it doesn't "sound right"

Tools to Try

- Generate as many sensory details as possible, such as color and specific characteristics of people.
- Put people in, even if the topic is impersonal.
- Write about your feelings on the topic – think about some aspect of the topic you care about.
- Use humor and subtle wit.
- Freewrite for an allotted amount of time, such as ten minutes, and resist revising.
- Jot down or list impressions about your topic.
- Include background material or anything about the past to frame your experience.

ESFPs:

Tendencies

- like to make something new out of something already existing, such as adapting new words to an old song
- are adept at drawing on their experience
- relate well to audience, even at the beginning of a writing project
- can juggle many ideas at once
- accept instruction readily and will follow an established form
- can see humor in almost anything

Troublespots

- may be reluctant to try new techniques, such as clustering
- may gather too much material from books if the subject is unfamiliar or involves research
- may depend too much on others' ideas if the subject is abstract, such as philosophy
- may "boilerplate" too readily – not inclined to reinvent the wheel
- may be inappropriately frivolous when the topic is serious
- may be overwhelmed by large projects
- may put off starting because writing is essentially introverted
- may start editing sentences too early because revising gives them immediate, concrete results
- may use too many quotations because quotes are concrete data to organize the piece around

Tools to Try

- Visualize your audience concretely. (Picture a particular person for whom you are writing.)
- Freewrite about something familiar or use your own experience just to get started.
- Use jokes, anecdotes, or anything else that is entertaining.
- Use active imagination dialogues to get an authentic sense of speech.
- Write quickly without too much reflection.
- Share ideas often and openly with someone you trust.
- Jot down your quick responses to your environment.
- Do something active if bogged down or work in short intervals.

ISFPs:

Tendencies

- need some contact with the natural world
- are good at describing the natural world
- are good at taking in nuances about their environment
- can describe in detail those items they have touched
- seek to please a team leader or mentor
- take instruction readily, but need to reflect on it
- have a strong "internal dialogue"
- need to include their values in their writing
- understand by doing rather than by explanations

Troublespots

- may give in too easily to the demands of others
- may not have confidence in their writing

- may be reluctant to share their writing with people they don't know well
- may become blocked by harsh feedback
- may be too understated even when their feelings are strong
- may become stuck if they have not experienced their topic
- may become confused or put off by long explanations
- may struggle with dry theory or argument

Tools to Try

- Find a trusted friend or mentor for feedback.
- If stuck, do something physical.
- Look at art, or make a piece of art, to free blocks and to generate material.
- Start by describing your office or your boss if you have to write about a technical or business topic.
- Dream outside in nature to get started.
- Freewrite or try an active imagination dialogue to get your internal dialogue on paper.
- Consult an established model for ideas.
- Avoid too much structure, such as notecards or outlines.

Sensing Thinking: ST

ESTJs:

Tendencies

- can make their own schedules to meet deadlines
- are good at collecting facts, details, and supporting data
- can see the flaws or inconsistencies in arguments
- are good at following instructions for a writing project
- are comfortable with business topics
- know when to limit research or stop gathering information
- can take strong stands
- perform best when they can see tangible results

Troublespots

- may get stuck when the topic is personal or requires feelings
- may not consider all the angles
- may judge their work too soon
- may dismiss theory, unusual ideas, or creative techniques
- may move on too quickly to the next stage in their drive to meet the deadline early
- may be uninspired if the topic isn't practical

Tools to Try

- View your freewrite as a tool to later form your thesis or focus.
- Find some practical use for the topic.
- List or jot down important ideas on notecards.
- Include concrete details and descriptions.
- If the topic is personal, freewrite about it objectively.
- If the topic is creative or fiction, find a model for ideas.
- List ideas sequentially or step-by-step.

ISTJs:
Tendencies
- like to pay attention to the senses, particularly the visual
- like to write sequentially, such as step-by-step
- like to group and categorize and can see parts quickly
- like to plan in their heads
- like a model to get started
- can generate ample detail, facts, and supporting data
- have an innate sense of when enough information has been gathered

Troublespots
- may cite too many "experts" to back up ideas
- may dislike personal topics or the abstract
- may not consider audience or the need to be tactful, particularly when irritated
- may become too immersed in detail
- may be "picky" when working in a group
- may "boilerplate" even when it isn't appropriate
- may be dry or blunt in their zeal to be objective

Tools to Try
- Get clear directions before starting.
- Cluster to have a visual of the information and to generate more detail.
- Make a sketch or flow chart of major findings.
- Make graphs or tables to illustrate complex ideas.
- Jot down ideas or make a list after you have reflected.
- Don't consider audience in this stage, particularly if you have to write about your feelings.
- Just stop when you think you've spent enough time on this stage.

ESTPs:
Tendencies
- are adept at seeing essential information
- are comfortable with many details
- like to process data with their hands
- like to use the computer to move data around
- like and need visuals
- have a high need for action
- are good team players when collaborating on a writing project, as long as they don't feel constrained by too many rules
- are good at problem-solving and trouble-shooting
- can write in marathon sessions because of their perseverance

Troublespots
- may have trouble sitting still in the Dreamer Stage
- may be overwhelmed when writing long pieces
- may be reluctant to use new or unfamiliar techniques
- may edit prematurely, even on a freewrite, thus breaking their flow of thoughts
- may procrastinate or have trouble getting started

- may "boilerplate" inappropriately
- may have trouble writing in isolation

Tools to Try
- Give yourself small diversions during this stage.
- Gather information on the computer.
- Jot down or list details on notecards.
- Think of your freewrite as a tool for the first draft.
- Resist editing sentences at this stage, unless you are absolutely stuck.
- Cluster to gather even more details and to generate something visual.
- Make a flow chart of the information.
- Write objectively at first and fit the people in later.
- Use a tape recorder to generate ideas.

ISTPs:

Tendencies
- need hands-on tactile engagement with their projects
- are good at collecting many details
- like to gather background information
- like to gather the pertinent facts
- have excellent observation skills
- can understand the intricate inner workings of objects
- need to reflect on the direction of their writing
- need to work at their own pace
- write spontaneously with bursts of energy

Troublespots
- may not like working with a team on a writing project
- may not continue a writing project if they lose interest
- may be too argumentative with an authority figure in charge of the writing project
- may not consider audience
- may dislike writing about anything abstract or personal
- may not seek feedback from others
- may not follow directions

Tools to Try
- Cluster to tinker with the various pieces of information and to produce a visual of your ideas.
- Freewrite on background.
- Look for what is going on behind what you observe.
- Delve into how something works.
- Write when your energy level is high.
- Begin with the practical or some problem to be solved.
- Use dry wit or satire.
- Get away from distractions.
- Work on the computer to generate ideas.

Intuitive Feeling: NF

ENFJs:

Tendencies

- are voracious readers and prolific writers
- have a knack for persuasion
- are good at conversational language or dialogue
- can convey a clear meaning of a complex idea
- can sense how much time is needed for a project
- need to stay in contact with people to avoid getting stuck
- can capture the nuances of language

Troublespots

- may overpersonalize or overuse "I"
- may resist writing about the impersonal or topics that require emotional distance
- may make a premature decision about direction during this stage
- may seek more breadth than depth (have too many ideas)
- may try too hard to achieve graceful prose too early
- may want to limit brainstorming and force a structure too quickly

Tools to Try

- Work with others during this stage.
- Listen to conversations to gather information.
- Read as much as possible about the topic.
- Write in an entertaining and anecdotal style.
- Limit the amount of time spent on generating ideas.
- Freewrite often and quickly.
- Cluster to come up with associations and figurative language.
- Play with words and connect them to ideas.
- Write persuasively and take a stand.
- Use active imagination dialogues to capture conversation and to get into the heads of the audience or characters.
- Use a tape recorder for ideas.

INFJs:

Tendencies

- need to feel closely connected to their topic
- can sense how much time is needed to generate ideas
- can connect seemingly disconnected information
- have flashes of insight
- can come up with many ideas quickly
- are original thinkers
- like to share their visions with others through writing
- like to write in a narrative style
- have a low need for supervision

Troublespots

- may judge something prematurely
- may not get motivated unless they feel the writing project is connected to their values
- may be too abstract without enough concrete examples
- may have trouble with a technical or impersonal topic
- may want to polish a first draft
- may get blocked in their drive to find just the right word

Tools to Try

- Freewrite to make a discovery about meaning.
- Write about feelings even if the topic is impersonal.
- Use active imagination dialogues to associate with your characters' struggles and to come up with quotes.
- Cluster a feeling or a person to come up with associations.
- Ask "what if" questions.
- Reflect, list, and cluster to come up with answers to those questions.
- Make a list of favorite words or synonyms.

ENFPs:

Tendencies

- are creative, original, and insightful
- can come up with many possibilities and ideas
- can put the spoken word into their writing
- have a feel for how the piece will sound, even in a freewrite
- can relate well to audience
- are natural "dreamers"
- can write fluently about anything that inspires them

Troublespots

- may procrastinate, especially if the writing project is impersonal
- may not feel inspired to get past the Dreamer Stage
- may misjudge deadlines and the amount of time needed to push on
- may try to work past their physical limits when inspired
- may attempt impossibly large writing projects
- may get restless or blocked working in isolation
- may be too optimistic rather than realistic in their approach

Tools to Try

- Get started early, preferably when most inspired.
- Allow as much time as needed for the Dreamer Stage in order to try out creative approaches.
- Cluster to come up with even more possibilities.
- Use active imagination dialogues to get a feel for the spoken word, intonation, and voice.
- Freewrite to convey voice and to get the overall impression or big picture early.
- Generate ideas at the computer or gather information on the Internet.
- Talk into a tape recorder to generate ideas.
- Write a "grabber" introduction to get off to a dramatic start.
- Put the people in, even if the topic is technical.

INFPs:

Tendencies

- are capable of and need highly creative and unique approaches
- need large blocks of uninterrupted time to concentrate
- like to look for meaning and implications behind the facts
- like to follow their own inner rhythm
- can generate many ideas quickly
- can "get in the flow" when creating

Troublespots

- may underestimate how much time is needed for a writing project
- may lose interest if they aren't in control of the project
- may get stuck if the topic is impersonal or too logical
- may try to include too much material
- may get overwhelmed by the breadth of the topic
- may try to perfect the project too soon
- may see no need to get the facts "right"

Tools to Try

- Cluster to come up with connections and combinations.
- Use alliteration, rhyme, hyperbole, and metaphor in your free-writes.
- Start in the middle rather than with an introduction.
- Use active imagination dialogues to get into the mind of the character.
- Write about your feelings, or personal values, even if the topic is technical or dry.
- Lower your standards – for now.
- If you can't find the right word, move on.
- Seek feedback from a trusted friend or colleague, even if it feels like criticism.

Intuitive Thinking: NT

ENTJs:

Tendencies

- are organized, logical, and efficient
- compare their writing to the standard and then act on their own conclusion
- are confident in both speaking and writing
- like to start with a sense of direction
- can see flaws in an argument
- like for their writing to serve a purpose
- like to be fully in charge of a writing project
- are comfortable with the conceptual and abstract

Troublespots

- may hesitate to seek others' feedback
- may not gather enough information in their zeal to come to closure
- may get locked into their topics prematurely without leaving room for the unexpected
- may not consider audience reaction
- may take charge inappropriately when collaborating with others

- Cluster to see the connections and associations and then look for the underlying order.
- Write about structures behind complex systems, such as the inner workings of the human body.
- Insert analogies, metaphorical language, and symbols.
- Write with a sense of authority.
- Gather ideas for your conclusion.
- Think of purpose in this stage.
- List and jot down the details that make up the whole.
- Gather information on the Internet.

INTJs:

Tendencies

- quickly see the big picture or the direction of a writing project
- can focus on the task at hand
- are good at deciphering technical material
- can cut through unnecessary information when gathering ideas
- have a logical approach
- are drawn to maps, graphs, charts, tables, and illustrations
- are quick to see flaws in a project or an idea

Troublespots

- may close their minds prematurely
- may be too skeptical
- may not spend the time needed on the Dreamer Stage
- may disregard material that isn't rational
- may have trouble writing on a personal topic
- may not use creative approaches that seem "touchy-feely" or esoteric (such as clustering or writing dialogues)

Tools to Try

- Write the conclusion first.
- Jot down or list ideas to get a sense of the logic behind the topic.
- Freewrite to see the coherent whole.
- Think of the cluster as a mind-map akin to a model of the mind.
- Spend less time on this stage with the idea of returning to it later to develop the writing project.
- Look up definitions and use your wide vocabulary.
- Gather graphs, tables, charts and other visuals.

ENTPs:

Tendencies

- can generate large amounts of data
- perceive patterns quickly, even in clusters and freewrites
- prefer the plan to the finished product

- are good at seeing the big picture
- like visuals, such as charts and graphs
- are imaginative, autonomous, and original
- like to be playful in their dreaming
- see possibilities quickly

Troublespots
- may not be energized to dream until the deadline looms
- may not like to sit still long enough to dream
- may fail to generate background material because they are so forward-looking
- may generate too many options for topics
- may have plans that are too elaborate for others if the writing project is collaborative
- may not follow a team leader in a collaborative project
- may be impatient with perceived incompetence

Tools to Try
- Talk with others as much as possible during this stage.
- Cluster quickly to come up with many associations and images.
- Generate details around the pattern as soon as it emerges.
- Insert wit, puns, and clever wordplay.
- Read your plans aloud or into a tape-recorder.
- Dream at the computer or gather information on the Internet.
- Gather material for charts, graphs, and illustrations.
- Dream up your own techniques for this stage.

INTPs:

Tendencies
- need time to reflect before putting pen to paper
- need their own space and independent writing projects
- like to write about complex problems
- are quick to spot flaws in arguments
- like to use wry humor in their writing
- like to gather a lot of material
- can work for hours at a time on a subject that interests them

Troublespots
- may not enjoy writing with a team
- may be too theoretical for a lay audience
- may ignore others' ideas, particularly if they are based on the "irrational" or can't be proved
- may have trouble with personal topics
- may be tempted to organize too early in their zeal to come up with underlying order
- may not like to view writing as having separate stages since they are capable of writing the whole piece in marathon sessions

Tools to Try
- Dream at the computer or research on the Internet.
- Cluster to produce a network of connecting lines and associations.
- Use metaphors, imagery, and other figurative language.

- Treat the project as a problem to be solved.
- Use active imagination dialogues to come up with strategies and solutions.
- Write lengthy freewrites.
- Allow yourself to dream until you come up with the underlying order and then go on to the next stage, returning to the Dreamer Stage later if you need more ideas.

Chapter Five:
The Designer

As you look back over the Dreamer Stage, you get a sense of its chaos. That's okay, because creativity often feels chaotic at the beginning. But at some point, you have to give form to the formless, and when you do, you move from the Dreamer to the Designer. Unfortunately, the Designer Stage is when the terror starts for many writers.

Just thinking about the jumble of notes, ideas, and information you gathered during the Dreamer Stage can cause anxiety. And when you start trying to organize this amorphous mass into a shape, you make several discoveries:

1. You have no idea how to begin.
2. You can think of a dozen ways to begin but they all lead to dead ends.
3. You were a complete fool to have thought this topic was a good idea in the first place.
4. You have gathered far too much material, but you haven't gathered nearly enough of the right material.
5. Miss Prissy, your high school English teacher, still lives in an apartment of your brain saying: "I want to see a complete, detailed outline before you start to write."
6. You would much rather be installing dashboard covers eight hours a day on the Pontiac assembly line in Detroit.

By this time, your brain has turned into a Tilt-a-Whirl carnival ride that won't stop spinning!

You can take some of the confusion out of the Designer Stage by thinking about your dream house. If you've decided that a contemporary house is what you want, then that house will probably be focused around cathedral ceilings, straight lines, hardwood floors, and sliding glass doors to let light in. You get a sense of its theme as you plan this house because the parts begin to form a big picture.

In fact, "big picture" is a key descriptive word for the Designer Stage. Read over the words in the second column of the chart and add any others that you feel relate to the Designer.

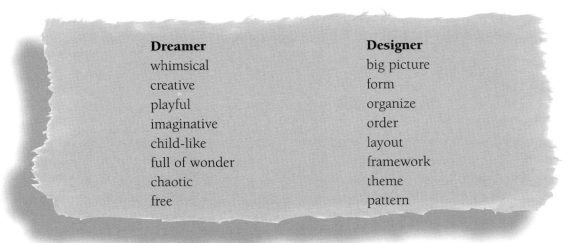

Dreamer	Designer
whimsical	big picture
creative	form
playful	organize
imaginative	order
child-like	layout
full of wonder	framework
chaotic	theme
free	pattern

Why the Designer Stage is Important

Most simply, the Designer Stage is where you decide what order in which to present your ideas and information. All writing needs order because order holds a piece together and helps the reader follow the material. To decide on the order, you need to know what you want to convey. What is this piece about? Can you state it in one sentence? What is your purpose? Do you want to inform, persuade, complain, evoke an emotional experience, entertain, express, tell a story, inspire, uplift, or comfort? Be as specific as possible.

Think, too, about the context for what you're writing. Is it for a professional journal, a church newsletter, a travel magazine? Closely connected to context is audience. Who will read this piece, and what is important to them? What do they care about, and what do they want to know? What questions would they ask? What do you want to happen in your readers?

The Designer Stage helps provide coherence for your readers (and for yourself). If the piece isn't easy to understand, your readers will give up. If you don't have a structure for all your ideas, then you will give up. Having a structure – whether it's an image or step-by-step instructions – keeps the piece flowing for both you and your readers.

Presenting the information sequentially can go a long way toward providing coherence. Sequence of presentation is how you stage the information and present it for your readers. If the readers need a definition before a description, for example, then that sequence is important.

Without sequence, the writer's ideas are like a crowd of people trying to get through a turnstyle – the ideas simply clog the opening and nothing gets through. With sequence, you provide an itinerary for your readers, a roadmap that keeps the reader from getting lost and frustrated. Sequence is comforting to readers because they know where they are and where they're going. Since ideas in the mind are not organized sequentially, but randomly, readers need the order that sequence provides to help them see what is there or what is missing.

In providing sequence, you might consider some key questions: What do the readers need to know first, second, third, etc.? What is the most important point? How can you present the information so that the readers can retain it? How can you present the material so that the ideas aren't swamped?

Writing down your responses to these questions can be indispensable in helping you organize because they give you a rough draft for you to develop and refine later. Once you have a rough draft, you feel relief because you can sense some kind of organization of your ideas.

What is Organization?

Organization is essentially about the relationship between the whole and its parts. Almost all organization involves analysis (breaking down the whole into some or all of its parts) and synthesis (finding the whole that a selection of parts fits into).

For example, if you're writing about the question of whether to require airbags in all automobiles, it could be part of the larger issues of automobile safety, child protection, or the role of the government. Then consider the sub-parts of the whole: the history of airbags, technology of airbags, current and proposed rules, statistical studies of airbags and their effect on injuries and deaths, case examples of lives saved or lost. When readers can see how the parts make up the whole, they are more likely to accept your premise.

Organization also involves unity. It is difficult to organize disparate elements until you find what unites them — what they have in common. What they have in common may be that they are opposites, but that still provides a unity. Trying to organize a piece that lacks unity is virtually impossible.

The Designer Stage doesn't have a clear beginning or end; rather, it describes a function that doesn't stop until the piece is published or the letter is mailed. Start by realizing that you probably won't know how to organize your material until you try several possibilities. Someone has suggested that the "trial" method really means "try-all."

Part of what's overwhelming at this stage is that there seem to be infinite possibilities for organizing the material, but you want to find just the right one for your content and purpose. It may help, then, to find the organizational structure inherent in the material.

Take a deck of cards, for example. How would you organize the cards? By suit? By color? In ascending numerical order? In descending numerical order? In alternating patterns of color or number? This card analogy suggests that organizing often involves finding and choosing a pattern.

Choosing a Pattern of Organization

Some of the patterns here may be appropriate for the piece as a whole while others may help you organize a section of the piece. As you look over them, think about the ones that you most often choose. This will give you an idea of the ones best suited to your personality type.

1. Chronological: This pattern is appropriate when you're writing up a trip report and your audience simply needs to know what happened when. It may also work in a history report when you're cataloging dates. Narratives and stories use chronological order to provide sequence of events. This pattern sometimes includes a past, present, future structure when you want to give background (past), status quo (present), and projections (future).

2. General to specific: This pattern starts with an umbrella statement, and all of the information that follows depends on that statement. The material gets increasingly more detailed with, say, a statistic or a quotation. By the end of the piece, the reader fully understands the general statement because of the details that back it up.

3. Specific to general: This pattern reverses the preceding one. The facts, details, quotes, statistics, and examples lead to a general statement. Not used as often as "general to specific," this pattern may be appropriate in conveying unpopular information such as proposing a tax hike, supporting a controversial point of view, or relaying bad news. By the time the reader gets to the end, he or she may be more prone to accept "the bitter pill." This pattern is also used when the writer wants to create suspense. To create suspense, withhold the essential piece of information until the reader is almost begging for it and can't stop reading until he or she gets to it. Of course, mystery stories often use this pattern.

4. Images: This pattern is useful if you want to make an impact. Suppose, for example, you're writing a piece about your grandfather's general store. The piece may revolve around the image of the glass counter where all the brightly colored candy enticed you as a child. The kindly clerk stood behind the counter and asked you about your day. This counter had all sorts of interesting objects on it, such as a gumball machine and a jangling cash register. The image of the counter leaves readers with a picture in their heads and provides a focus for the piece.

5. Problem-solution: To use this pattern, ask yourself some key questions. What is the problem? What caused it; what are its roots? What would cure it? Would the solutions be economically feasible? Would the readers be open to them? Are they timely? Would they work? Problem-solution is the most common pattern in technical writing, but it will only be effective if readers are receptive to the solution.

6. Cause and effect or analysis: This pattern is similar to the preceding one except that it explores the causes of a problem rather than the solutions. Be sure that you follow sound reasoning in your analysis. For example, if you're writing about welfare, you might start with the larger issue of poverty as the root cause that led to setting up the

system of welfare. Then you might explore the effects of welfare and the issues that led to dismantling major parts of the system. Be sure that point one leads to point two which logically leads to point three. If you assert that welfare has failed because the recipients were lazy, then that reasoning is faulty.

7. Compare-contrast: Before you can take two things apart, they have to be brought together. The adage "You can't compare apples and oranges" applies here. Perhaps you're trying to help a reader make a decision between a Honda Civic or a Honda Accord. When you compare (find similarities) or contrast (state differences), be sure you come up with criteria. For example, one computer might make a better purchase than another because of the criteria of cost, speed, and reliability of its manufacturer. Advantages-disadvantages also fits under this pattern, as does positive-negative.

8. Theme emerging from the material: "Lesson learned" could be a natural theme emerging from the material you've gathered in the Dreamer Stage. Perhaps you're writing a narrative about the time you ran away from home. Rather than simply detailing events chronologically, focus the material around the main lesson learned from that experience. Writing about the lesson learned takes the narrative from the "what" to the "so what."

9. Acronyms: This pattern would be more appropriate for shorter pieces because of the danger of over-working the acronym. Here's the way acronyms work. A humorist once told a group that if you think "L-A-U-G-H" in a difficult situation, you'll be less stressed. (L stands for "Let go," A for "Attitude," U for "You," G for "Go for it," and H for "Humor.") I once wrote an article for a newsletter about flunking "L-A-U-G-H" at the dentist's office. (Look at the back of this chapter for the article.) That acronym provided a built-in structure for my theme: that some situations aren't funny, no matter what.

10. Who, what, where, when, why, and how: This pattern is the journalist's approach. It works well in memo writing and in reports when the reader wants information without analysis. It's the most straight-forward of all the patterns and provides an objective, no-nonsense approach.

11. Spatial: This pattern is useful in writing descriptions. When you organize the paper spatially, you take the reader from left to right, top to bottom, or front to back. The spatial pattern gives readers a firm sense of order as they try to visualize the scene or object.

12. The Speech Format: This pattern generally follows the advice, "Tell them what you're going to tell them (introduction), tell them (two to five body paragraphs), and tell them what you told them (conclusion)." This pattern is especially helpful for beginning writers because it generally cannot fail the organization test.

A note about paragraphs: In the Designer Stage, paragraphs are best called "units of ideas." These units of ideas will provide a better focus for the larger design if they have a guiding statement of purpose, such as a topic sentence. Place the topic sentence at the beginning of the unit of ideas.

How to Keep Improving your Organization

Remember that in the Designer Stage, it's perfectly okay to go back and gather more information as you organize your piece. At this point, the Dreamer and Designer Stages interact with one another. For example, you may want to take one idea from a cluster in the Dreamer Stage as you focus more and more finely on theme. That is, one part of your cluster (perhaps an image) may serve as the pattern of organization for your piece. You cluster that image again to gather more specific associations.

You may also want to try focusing one of your freewrites. Freewriting was presented in the Dreamer Stage as a way to "mind dump." In a focused freewrite, you follow all the guidelines for freewriting, but you write on a part of your piece that you've decided to keep.

In his article, "Making Freewriting More Productive," Mark Reynolds talks about how freewriting can help you organize your piece (24: pp. 81-82). Reynolds suggests making a list of what you consider to be the main points in the freewrite. Does a pattern emerge from the list? As you list, other points will probably come to you.

Reynolds also suggests expressing in one sentence the main point (or thesis) of your freewrite. If one isn't obvious, is it implied? Do key words or phrases recur in the freewrite? These can be clues to the main point. You may even want to go back and cluster key words because they can lead to an organizational pattern.

Try applying a preliminary outline after you've finished one or more drafts of the piece. A preliminary outline can help you see where points are missing. Use headings to emphasize the organization. Headings not only help the reader, but also help the writer see how the main sections flow.

If you decide to write a preliminary outline to help you organize, you might want to learn to use the outline feature on your word processor. The better outliners are easy and versatile. You can instantly arrange, change, add, delete, show, and hide levels. The real benefit of using an outliner on your word processor is that everything can be easily changed and therefore be tentative. The outliner lets you see what you have, and it adds parts easily.

An old standby that still works is writing all your ideas and subtopics on separate index cards. You then try arranging the index cards in different ways until you find a pattern that works. Index cards allow you to remain flexible while you're searching for just the right strategy for organizing your piece.

You might want to study the organization of others' writing, especially those you admire or enjoy. This will allow you to learn from professionals and will make you generally more aware of organization. (You'll have a chance in Chapter Eleven to work with models of professional writing.) The table of contents in books can also help you see a variety of organizational approaches.

Keep in mind that, for most writers, the Designer Stage is actually for writing the first draft. Everything you wrote before was for gathering information. This first draft provides a direction for your piece and helps you to see the pattern that unifies the information.

Try some or all of the exercises for practice in using the organizational patterns suggested in this chapter. In Chapter Six, you'll find more specific suggestions for writers with your particular personality type.

Exercises:

1. Think of an issue at work, such as a new policy. Start by writing the pros and cons of the policy and then write a short draft using compare and contrast. Feel free to use another pattern of organization if it better suits the issue you choose.
2. Write a brief narrative about a turning point in your life. First, detail the events chronologically, and then pick out a focus that would organize the narrative. (The focus might be "lesson learned.")
3. Think of a central image from your childhood home or town. It might be a tree you climbed, a favorite hiding place, or a favorite toy. Write a quick draft organizing all of your thoughts around this image.
4. Analyze an issue by looking at its causes. Environmental issues fit nicely with this pattern. What caused the pollution in a river or lake in your town or state? What led to the disappearance of a certain species in your part of the country?
5. Think of a problem at work or in some other phase of your life. It could be something like balancing your monthly budget, disciplining a teenager, or managing your time. Consider some of the causes of the problem and sketch out some feasible solutions.

Note: "The Whole Tooth" illustrates how an acronym can organize a piece of writing (point #9 under "Choosing a Pattern of Organization.")

The Whole Tooth

Maybe it stems from my being a pain avoider on the Enneagram, but I definitely have a dental phobia. Whenever I have to go to the dentist, I'm reminded of the boy who telephoned the dentist's office and said, "I'm supposed to make an appointment." "I'm sorry," replied the nurse, "but the doctor is out of town." "Thank you," said the boy. "When will he be out of town again?" So when I had an appointment to get an inlay on July 25, I thought to myself, "This is a situation that calls for humorizing. What can I do to give it a little levity? Levitate out of the chair? Banter with the dentist while my mouth is contorted in every possible direction and probed with all kinds of sharp instruments? Visualize Jesse Helms at a New Age church? Beg for laughing gas?"

Laugh — that was it! I would put into practice Alan Klein's suggestion to think L-A-U-G-H: L standing for "Let go," A for "Attitude," U for "You," G for "Go for it" (or was it "Get a Grip"?), and H for "The Healing Power of Humor."

After being numbed by three shots of novocaine and hooked up to laughing gas, I was all set for the ordeal. "Let go," I thought to myself. "Relax. Visualize a peaceful scene." Then the dentist came in. "The reason for the wait," she said, "is that we can't find your inlay. We think it's here, but under the name of Linda Moore. Somebody at the lab mislabeled it. But don't worry; we'll just try it on for size and if it fits, it's yours." By this time I was about as relaxed as Al Gore singing "Twist and Shout."

O.K., I thought, "attitude." I've got to change my attitude. Mistakes happen. So what if I might be wearing Linda Moore's inlay. Just go with the flow. "Well," said the dentist. "It seems you have just a little decay on the tooth right beside the inlay. May as well go ahead and fill it while you're numb. It's small — you won't know the difference," she said as she set the drill on "high squeal." "Get me some head phones quick," I yelled. "This drill is really a high tech mosquito from another planet! I saw him eating people in 'Independence Day.'"

"U" big baby, I thought. U are the problem. It's just like Alan Klein said. U are your own worst enemy. The only person U can change is Urself. "Now," said my dentist. "We're almost through. All we have left is this clamp to wedge between your teeth to make some space." U blankity, blank, blank! U lied. U said this wouldn't hurt. I was rapidly flunking LAUGH. It was time to get back on track.

All right — "G." Go for it. Get a grip. Grow up. "You're doing fine," I heard the dentist say. "Now bite down hard. No — harder. We've got to get that baby cemented in there. Uh, oh. It's a little loose. I surely do hope this inlay is the right one." Well, G. D., I thought. Get real. I'd better go on to "H" and think of some humor before I hyperventilate.

Jokes. That's it. I'll think of some old dentist jokes to lighten me up. Q: "What time is your dentist appointment?" A: "Toothhurty." Ha ha. "Never go to a dentist whose office plants have died." Hee hee. Nope — it wasn't working. All I wanted was to get the H out of there.

Well, I tried, but truth to tell, some situations just can't be humorized no matter what. I have a dental phobia, and I'll never recover. My 80 year-old aunt summed it up just right: "I was supposed to go in for a root canal," she said, "but fortunately, I had a heart attack."

(Written for Carolina Health & Humor Association, 1996)

Chapter Six:
Using Your Preferences in the Designer Stage

Since organizing material can be the hardest stage of the writing process, it's essential to approach this stage without feeling overwhelmed. This chapter should help. Start by looking up your personality type; the types are grouped according to the cognitive functions, as they were in Chapter Four.

When you find your type preferences, read over the "tendencies." Remember that "tendencies" indicate possible, rather than absolute, characteristics. For example, if you prefer perceiving, you tend to "see the entire field in an inexact way." You might remember from Chapter One that this means you prefer to use the right brain hemisphere when looking over your environment. The right brain is more global. "Global" here doesn't mean "big picture," which is an intuitive characteristic; rather, it means taking a sweeping look over the "field," which refers to your environment. Therefore, perceiving types may have more trouble narrowing their topic and focusing on a theme.

If you prefer judging, you tend to "see one part of the field in an exact way." This means that as you look over your environment, you prefer to use the left brain hemisphere, which is more focused. "Focused" here means that you can zero in on one part of your environment. Therefore, judging types may focus on a theme before considering other issues and options.

Feeling types may also have special problems in the Designer stage. In general, feeling types have more trouble with organization than thinking types do. One reason is that thinking types tend to be more adept at classifying, sorting, and finding a framework; another reason is that thinking types are generally not as reluctant to cut information. Feeling types are usually more emotionally invested in their material and may not want to let any of it go.

The section on "troublespots" will build awareness of the pitfalls associated with your type. Some of the tendencies or troublespots in this chapter may overlap with those you read about in Chapter Four. That's because the Dreamer and Designer Stages weave in and around one another, like a dance. When you are creating, the writing process is more circular than linear.

"Tools to Try" will give you some concrete suggestions for handling your troublespots. They are not in any particular order because you may want to pick out just one or two to try. They can be useful for times when you find yourself falling into the trap of procrastination or avoidance in the Designer Stage. The tools can help get you back on track.

You might want to go back to the exercises at the end of Chapter Five as you read over the suggestions for your type in this chapter. The exercises may help you choose the approach that is most comfortable for you.

Sensing Feeling: SF

ESFJs:

Tendencies
- see one part of the field in an exact way
- act before reflecting

- relate well to audience
- are structured and focused
- plan and organize well
- need a tried and true format or a model
- like sequential patterns to organize
- seek closure early
- like to feel in control of their writing projects

Troublespots
- may not be inclusive enough
- may be too sentimental in their expression
- may have trouble analyzing
- may prefer to talk about their topic rather than write
- may lack originality
- may "boilerplate" or use a model inappropriately
- may need too much feedback for certainty

Tools to Try
- Write a preliminary outline to get a sense of structure.
- Write about the past and link it to personal experience.
- Focus around a feeling or a value.
- Choose a family member or a tradition as a part of your topic.
- Get feedback often from a trusted colleague or mentor.
- Write a conclusion early to get a sense of closure.
- Picture a friend or family member as your audience.
- Plan and organize your time to feel in control.
- Cite authorities to get a feel for being on the right track.
- Use a piece that you admire as a beginning model.
- Write in a narrative style.

ISFJs:
Tendencies
- see one part of the field in an exact way
- reflect before acting; need quiet for concentration
- like to write about tradition or the past
- are structured and organize their time well
- are consistent and responsible about deadlines
- enjoy collecting facts, especially about history
- like to follow guidelines and instructions
- like sequential patterns
- need clear instructions from a mentor or supervisor
- have a warm and quietly humorous tone

Troublespots
- may not try something "new"
- may dislike composing on the computer until it is familiar

- may be reluctant to share writing with others
- may have trouble with analysis
- may have trouble with theory or the abstract
- may not see connections
- may not have confidence in their writing

Tools to Try

- Focus as soon as possible.
- Focus on family, experience, ritual, or tradition.
- Keep scrapbooks and write from them.
- Focus on feelings and values.
- Spend time reflecting and observing.
- Use a model or a familiar framework.
- Write with warmth and humor.
- Start with the facts.
- Write in chronological order or past-present-future.
- Use compare-contrast to tap your natural ability to see contrasts.
- Write a preliminary outline, or at least a guideline.
- Write the piece as a letter to someone you know well.

ESFPs:

Tendencies

- see the entire field in an inexact way
- want their writing to lead to action
- are contextual
- want their writing to resonate with audience or be entertaining
- like to use dialogue, quotes, and humor
- like to write about personal experience
- get "on a roll" and then draft quickly
- like short paragraphs
- like to use chronological patterns, such as past-present-future

Troublespots

- may have trouble seeing the big picture
- may gather too much information and then feel overwhelmed when it is time to focus
- may dislike writing dry reports without personal examples
- may edit sentences prematurely
- may have trouble with conclusions
- may "boilerplate" or adapt to existing formats instead of using a fresh approach
- may have trouble writing in isolation

Tools to Try

- Avoid spinning wheels by reflecting — just start writing.
- Read the draft aloud to hear how it sounds.
- Ask, "What do you want this piece of writing to do? Entertain, inspire, motivate, inform?"
- Put your topic into a contextual framework, such as the current season or holiday.
- Choose past-present-future or another chronological pattern of organization.

- Choose compare-contrast to tap your natural ability to see similarities.
- Write conversationally or anecdotally.
- Delay writing the conclusion.
- Write out a complete draft to discover theme.
- Picture the audience as a trusted friend or family member.

ISFPs:

Tendencies

- see the entire field in an inexact way
- internalize experience
- reflect before acting
- need private time away from distraction
- need to "feel" before forming words
- like hands-on experiences to write from
- write best from a model
- like their writing to have a practical purpose
- like using sequential patterns to organize

Troublespots

- may find it hard to share experiences with others
- may gather too much information
- may have trouble focusing
- may try too hard to please the audience
- may have trouble with "voice"
- may dislike dry, analytical reports
- may have trouble with logical analysis

Tools to Try

- Write as naturally as possible to tap a voice.
- Reflect often; listen to your internal dialogue.
- Find a mentor or a guide to give you specific instruction.
- Experience the natural world while focusing.
- Put your topic into a contextual framework, such as the current season or holiday.
- Focus around a color, smell, or texture.
- Write about natural themes, such as plants, water, or animals.
- Use a model to write from.
- Use a chronological pattern or write about a "lesson learned."
- Be inclusive at this stage.

Sensing Thinking: ST
ESTJs:

Tendencies

- see one part of the field in an exact way
- act before reflecting

- like order and organization
- are good at meeting deadlines
- like to categorize and sort
- like to use step-by-step processing and sequential patterns
- like a routine way of doing things
- like to include case studies of theoretical concepts
- are good at paperwork and details
- like formulas, handbooks, and guidelines
- like to write "how to" papers
- are adept at logical analysis

Troublespots
- may be closed to new ideas
- may be inflexible with schedules
- may not consider audience
- may sound like a bureaucrat
- may have a harsh tone
- may lose patience with "fuzzy thinking" or strained analogies
- may dislike using feeling words or personal pronouns

Tools to Try
- Write about procedures or directions rather than people.
- Find the focus or structure early.
- Write the conclusion early.
- Write a preliminary outline.
- Argue your point.
- Use many details.
- Describe and prescribe.
- Include case studies.
- Use problem-solution or chronology as an organizational pattern.
- Use notecards to organize your material.

ISTJs:
Tendencies
- see one part of the field in an exact way
- focus on one thing at a time
- reflect before acting
- are sequential thinkers
- are visual; like to use charts and graphs
- like to use computers for drafting
- are efficient and organized
- are economical and resourceful
- are predictable and reliable
- like to plan mentally
- like standards, formulas, and guidelines

- like facts and details
- value clarity of format, such as headings

Troublespots
- may "boilerplate" or lack originality
- may be too rigid in expectations
- may delay writing, preferring to plan mentally first
- may be reluctant to change "what works"
- may not consider audience
- may use dry prose or be too analytical
- may not see the big picture or the theme in all the data

Tools to Try
- Include graphs, tables, charts, and other visuals.
- Include facts, details, and illustrations.
- Write objectively.
- Compare and contrast numbers, sizes, weights, functions, and colors.
- Write a preliminary outline.
- Categorize information into headings.
- Make a hard copy early so that the information can be seen.
- Use a tried and true format or model to write from.
- Work in regular intervals.

ESTPs:

Tendencies
- see the entire field in an inexact way
- act before reflecting
- are contextual
- look for the action behind the idea
- are adept at moving pieces around
- can see what doesn't fit
- are adept at finding the right clues that make up the whole
- are good at reading their environment
- like short words and short assignments

Troublespots
- may be impatient or easily distracted
- may not like to write about personal topics
- may not consider audience
- may be overwhelmed by longer pieces of writing
- may not take the time to deal with the abstract
- may put off writing and not leave enough time

Tools to Try
- Start early, leaving enough time to develop a focus.
- Begin with a brief sketch or a short preliminary outline.
- Look for the essential clues that have emerged from the Dreamer Stage.

- Put these clues together to find a focus.
- Put these clues in context (according to whatever is going on at the time, such as a holiday or event).
- Include as many details as possible at this stage.
- Move things around on the computer.
- Focus around things or objects.
- Think of the writing as a puzzle — you're finding the pieces.
- Include charts, graphs, and illustrations.
- Show your audience how they can act on what you've written.

ISTPs:

Tendencies
- see the entire field in an inexact way
- reflect before acting
- are contextual
- are adept at reading their environment
- look for the idea behind the action
- are adept at seeing the parts of an object
- like background information
- are concise or direct in response
- learn best by doing

Troublespots
- may not like to undertake longer pieces of writing
- may need to take an object apart before writing about it
- may be too brief, terse, or blunt
- may not see the whole for the parts
- may not seek feedback, preferring to work alone
- may put off writing, preferring to collect data mentally
- may dislike paper work
- may defy authority and expectations
- may not like personal disclosure

Tools to Try
- Take photographs to write from.
- Label every part of an object you are describing.
- Give background information and details.
- Put the information and details in context (according to whatever is currently going on, such as a holiday or event).
- Write a short first draft with short paragraphs.
- Keep a notebook of observations and focus around one of them.
- Use the computer often to organize.
- Argue your point of view.
- Use irony and satire.
- Use problem-solution as an organizing pattern.

Intuitive Feeling: NF

ENFJs:

Tendencies

- see one part of the field in an exact way
- act before reflecting
- like collaboration in the writing process
- are focused and decisive
- are enthusiastic about their writing
- seek closure quickly
- like to use anecdotes or record conversations
- are persuasive and articulate
- enjoy humor
- are adept at finding associations

Troublespots

- may spend time talking rather than writing
- may come to closure too soon without considering other angles
- may need much outside stimulation during a writing project
- may neglect their own needs during projects
- may have trouble working alone
- may need to elaborate on key points
- may overpersonalize the piece of writing

Tools to Try

- Write the conclusion first but keep it flexible and open.
- Clarify the point behind your anecdotes.
- Balance your time between interacting and writing alone.
- Write to persuade.
- Write about values.
- Write longer paragraphs with more depth.
- Focus around an analogy or a metaphor.
- Write conversationally, using the first person.

INFJs:

Tendencies

- see one part of the field in an exact way
- reflect before acting
- have strong feelings and preferences
- seek meaning in the feelings
- can focus in depth
- enjoy speculating
- are adept at ordering information
- are adept at finding the one big idea
- are original and visionary
- are adept at writing in sections

Troublespots
- may be overly sensitive to audience and feedback
- may develop their ideas in too much isolation
- may have trouble cutting personally invested ideas
- may lack clarity or fail to use logical analysis
- may have trouble writing about impersonal topics
- may try too hard to be unique

Tools to Try
- Divide the writing into sections or parts.
- Incorporate your values and ideals into your writing.
- Seek feedback from a trusted friend or colleague.
- Avoid taking their feedback too personally.
- Write down visionary ideas.
- Write about people or strong feelings.
- Visualize the audience as a friend or mentor.
- Write formally at first.
- Give yourself time alone for reflection.
- Focus your draft around a central symbolic image.

ENFPs:
Tendencies
- see the entire field in an inexact way
- act before reflecting
- are adept at seeing possibilities and connections
- are adept at harmonizing seemingly dissimilar parts
- are sensitive to tone
- can read between the lines
- are inspired by outer events

Troublespots
- may find it hard to be critical
- may find routine writing deadly
- may need to be continually inspired
- may find it difficult to meet deadlines
- may drive themselves without regard to physical needs
- may juggle too many writing projects at once
- may dislike handling facts
- may disregard standard formats

Tools to Try
- Withdraw from the writing project periodically.
- Focus the writing project in a unique way.
- Think of each draft or stage as a deadline.
- Read the draft aloud to hear tone.
- Incorporate dialogue.

- Visualize and "talk" to the audience on paper.
- Discuss your writing often for inspiration.
- Write in a narrative or conversational style.
- Think of some way the writing can help people.

INFPs:
Tendencies
- see the entire field in an inexact way
- reflect before acting
- like to play with words
- have an innate feel for the piece of writing
- can combine seemingly disparate ideas or objects
- like to write poetry
- enjoy figurative language
- are imaginative in their approach
- need for the parts of the paper to fit together
- like to strive for elegance and smoothness in their prose

Troublespots
- may get hung up on introductions and conclusions
- may not present enough examples or facts to illustrate concepts
- may lack a clear focus
- may write rambling or inconclusive paragraphs
- may strive to be too elegant or imaginative in routine work
- may get discouraged if writing doesn't serve ideals
- may not seek feedback from others
- may agonize over word choice

Tools to Try
- Save introductions and conclusions for last.
- Begin writing in the middle.
- Engage personal values and feelings.
- Avoid spending too much time looking for the right word.
- Focus around a metaphor, an image, or an analogy.
- Find unique connections between parts.
- Visualize and connect with the audience.
- Write a lengthy first draft.
- Use a compare-contrast pattern to tap your natural ability to see combinations.

Intuitive Thinking: NT
ENTJs:
Tendencies
- see one part of the field in an exact way
- act before reflecting
- enjoy leading others

- are organized
- enjoy intellectual challenges
- can get to the point quickly
- can see the big picture
- like technical reports and manuals
- are adept at clarity
- are adept at conclusions
- are logical and coherent
- are adept at finding structure or underlying form
- like breaking the structure down into logical pieces

Troublespots
- may leave out the personal
- may be overly concerned with clarity and efficiency
- may seek out too much feedback and then not use it
- may be too blunt, terse, or critical
- may be too concise
- may not be concerned about connecting with audience
- may set standards that are too high
- may be overly confident or buck authority
- may lose interest if their writing doesn't serve a clear purpose

Tools to Try
- Write the conclusion early.
- Write a preliminary outline to find the underlying structure.
- Use cause-effect and problem-solution patterns of organization.
- Use logical analysis.
- Present the big picture in the introduction.
- Use metaphors, symbols, and analogies.

INTJs:

Tendencies
- see one part of the field in an exact way
- reflect before acting
- are original and independent thinkers
- are pragmatic
- like to plan mentally
- enjoy the closure of meeting deadlines on time or early
- place a high value on facts that fit into their concepts
- are logical and orderly
- enjoy systems and models

Troublespots
- may not listen to others' feedback
- may be too blunt or argumentative

- may not consider audience
- may not embrace accepted ideas
- may sound too "final"
- may place too high a value on the rational
- may need too much independence
- may become prematurely locked into their plans

Tools to Try

- Use visuals such as charts, graphs, and tables.
- Write the conclusion early.
- Use logical analysis.
- Leave out the personal in your first draft.
- Write about pragmatic concepts.
- Look for the relationship between the parts.
- Use logical sequence and orderly flow.
- View the writing as a "model."
- Develop a "system" for your writing.
- Look for facts that fit concepts.

ENTPs:

Tendencies

- see the entire field in an inexact way
- act before reflecting
- are adept at seeing patterns
- can see the big picture
- can handle large amounts of data
- are adept at abstract, logical reasoning
- are adept at problem-solving
- enjoy processing and planning
- like to use a new approach
- can be visionaries
- enjoy witty, playful humor

Troublespots

- may be restless with routine
- may need lots of action or stimulation to write
- may rebel against authority
- may be impatient with background material
- may seem argumentative or critical in tone
- may generate too many options
- may neglect the personal

Tools to Try

- Use charts, graphs, and other visuals.
- Talk to someone often during the writing process.
- Find a unique, challenging way of presenting your theme.
- Let your sense of recurring patterns guide your focus.

- Present the big picture in the introduction.
- Work on the computer to move parts around.
- Argue both your point of view and the opposition's.
- Put in as much data as possible.
- Use problem-solution as an organizing pattern.
- Use wit or satire.
- Seek the stimulation of the outside world often as you write.

INTPs:

Tendencies

- see the entire field in an inexact way
- reflect before acting
- have a strong sense of curiosity
- are adept at research
- are adept at problem-solving
- are analytical
- like independent projects and solitude
- enjoy writing on the computer
- have a wry sense of humor
- enjoy strategizing and finding patterns
- have a strong imagination
- like to write about the theoretical

Troublespots

- may dislike traditional approaches
- may make things too complex
- may write a too elaborate outline
- may be too abstract
- may become bored with the mundane
- may be cynical in tone
- may not seek feedback about their work

Tools to Try

- Draft on the computer.
- Allow plenty of time away from distractions.
- See the assignment as a problem to solve.
- Design your own strategy for the paper.
- Avoid formats or formulas.
- Use problem-solution as an organizing pattern.
- If you decide to outline, write a draft first.
- Engage logic and analysis.
- Use your wry sense of humor.
- Leave out the personal at first.
- Use metaphors, analogies, and figurative language.

Chapter Seven:

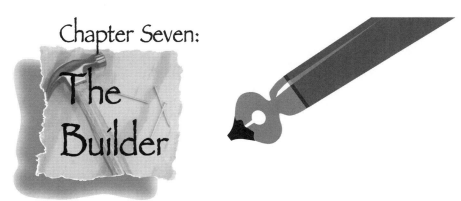

The Builder

Let's return to the house analogy. After you've laid the foundation of your house in the Dreamer and Designer Stages, you're ready to start the Builder Stage. Before the boards go up, you have a sense of overall layout, but the essentials are missing. The Builder Stage begins when you put the rooms together and add cabinets, sinks, closets, and perhaps a fireplace. It is up to the builder to supply the elements that give the house substance.

What words do you think of when you consider a builder's purpose? Look at the words under the Builder column and add any others that come to mind.

Dreamer	Designer	Builder
whimsical	big picture	construct
creative	form	add to
playful	organize	flesh out
imaginative	order	develop
child-like	layout	make
full of wonder	framework	put together
chaotic	theme	erect
free	pattern	carve

You may be a writer who tries to start at the Builder Stage. You want a near perfect first draft because then all you have to do is go back through it to cut and edit. The problem comes when you try to write for yourself and your audience all at once. A piece of writing must first be dreamed and designed in your natural way before it can be fleshed out to relate to those who will read it.

This stage is called "The Builder" because you're building content not only to improve the piece and make it more interesting but also to better communicate with other personality types. In your first drafts, you write from who you are and in your authentic voice; in your final drafts, you focus not only on self-expression but also on being understood by the reader.

Techniques for the Builder Stage

The Builder Stage, then, is about developing ideas and adding detail. The techniques that you'll read about in this chapter will help you do that. In the Dreamer Stage, you may have already gathered information on some of the techniques that you'll explore in this chapter; for example, if you're a sensing type, you have probably gathered some ideas for description or for examples. If you're an intuitive type, you may have thought of an analogy or an image. As you read over the techniques, consider which ones may not be so natural for you to use but may help you improve your piece and relate to different audiences.

Definition

Sometimes you need to include a definition to explain or clarify a term. An effective definition involves writing two parts: placing the term in a class or category and following it by an explanation of what it does within that class or category. Explaining what it does differentiates the term from other items in its class.

Here are some definitions that might help people new to type: "In general usage, people might equate 'sensing' with 'sensitive.' But in type language, the term 'sensing' refers to the perceiving function that gathers information primarily through the five senses. Similarly, people might equate 'intuition' with fortune-telling or guess-work. In type language, though, 'intuition' refers to the perceiving function that gathers information through inner knowing and insights that go beyond the five senses."

When you're providing a definition, be sure that you're precise in your word choice rather than circular and vague. Here's an example of an imprecise definition: "'Sensing' is what sensing types use when they are looking at the world." A precise and effective definition helps readers relate to new material.

In technical writing, definitions are often used for non-technical audiences, as in this example: "A paper micrometer is a small measuring instrument used to measure the thickness of a piece of paper. The micrometer, roughly twice as large as a regular stapler, has four main parts: the frame, the dial, the hand lever, and the piston" (26: p. 231). This definition is effective because it relates the unfamiliar (paper micrometer) to the familiar (stapler) and presents the different parts of the object.

If you're using a familiar word in a new way, you'll probably need to define it, particularly if the word is vague or abstract. "Love" is a common abstract word that may need defining because it has many levels. Perhaps you're using "love" to convey sentimental feelings or an attachment or even an infatuation. Or you might want to show how "tough love" is a special kind of love because it can result in the needed psychological growth of your loved one.

A definition is necessary if the reader would probably ask, "But what does the writer mean by …?" The decision to include a definition will likely depend on your audience's knowledge and experience — and on personality type, as you will see more clearly in the next chapter.

Description

How does "orange" differ from "pumpkin orange"? How does "rust" differ from "orange" or "red"? How does "black" differ from "midnight black"? And how does "grass" differ from "freshly cut grass"? By writing more detailed and precise descriptions, you will engage your readers and help them "see" your prose.

In her book *Wild Mind*, Natalie Goldberg shows how effective sensory description propels the reader into the prose and gives a sense of "being there" (8: p. 204).

"Hal is sitting in a steak house waiting for Sal. The waitress whizzes by, holding in her hand a white plate with a hamburger and lettuce and thin slice of tomato on the side. The lettuce and tomato are about to fall over, they are so close to the plate's rim, but they don't thanks to the adept grace of the red-haired waitress."

"The girl has red lips, white teeth, freckles brushed across her nose, eyes that hint at lilacs, and she just lifted her right eyebrow."

In more technical writing, writers often provide descriptive facts and details for their readers, such as measurements, weights, numbers, percentages, and statistics. Example: "The truck box size is an important factor because we frequently transport 4 ft by 8 ft sheets of wood. The box size of the Hauler at the floor is 3.5 ft by 6 ft. The box size of the X-200 at the floor is 4 ft by 8 ft. This factor means we should purchase the X-200" (26: p. 229).

Whether you're writing fiction, such as poetry and novels, or nonfiction, such as essays and technical reports, descriptive details are essential to building your content. The reader shouldn't have to guess the color of the girl's eyes or the size of the truck box. Anytime you suspect that your readers need more information, they probably do.

Step-by-Step Instructions

When readers need information quickly and concisely, numbered steps can be a useful way to build content and highlight important points. Numbered steps provide inherent organization, and they are most often used when you are illustrating how to do or make something, as in instructions.

Here are some guidelines for presenting instructions.

In the introduction:

1. Write a statement that tells what the instructions will enable the reader to do.
2. Define any vague or unfamiliar terms.
3. Provide a list of all materials needed to carry out the instructions.

In the body:

1. Begin numbering the steps.
2. Place the information in a sequential or logical order. This includes any "cautions"; the logical place for "cautions" is before the step to be carried out, not after.
3. Use command verbs, as I have done in these instructions. The understood subject of command verbs is "you." Using command verbs cuts down on wordiness and makes the prose more direct.
4. Include a, an, or the before your nouns. Removing them makes the sentences unclear.

For an example of a set of instructions, look back in Chapter One at "How to Find the Dominant." You'll also find a set of instructions in Chapter Nine: "Five Quick Ways to Improve Your Style."

Examples

Examples give readers concrete information to help them understand ideas or terms. Suppose I use the word "flamboyant" in a developmental English class and the students look back at me with blank faces. To help them grasp this new vocabulary word, I might use the example of the basketball player Dennis Rodman, who dyes his hair a different color for every game. Older readers may better relate to the example of Liberace, the pianist who wore jackets bedecked with sequins.

To state that there have been many changes in modes of transportation during the 20th century is a generalization that everyone agrees with. But to state that America has gone from the horse and buggy to the automobile to the airplane to rockets and space capsules in 100 years provides examples of the modes of transportation. Whenever I wanted concrete examples about changes in the 20th century, I would always ask my 98-year-old aunt. "It's mind-boggling," she would say. "It used to take a month for a letter to get here from another state, and now you can send one to Japan over the computer in a matter of minutes."

General (or new) ideas usually need examples. When writing about how feeling types differ from thinking types, I gave the example in Chapter One of the parents who were trying to decide whether or not to allow their 16-year-old daughter to go to a party. Without that example, you might not have fully grasped the difference.

Quotations

If not overused, quotations are an effective way to build content and add interest. They provide a human element to prose. The quotation from my aunt is a better way to make the point about examples than merely telling you that examples are important. Readers sit up and pay attention when they come across quotations.

Quotations also add credibility when you're arguing a point. If an expert in the field agrees with you, then your argument carries more weight. Suppose you're making an argument against capital punishment and you know that most of your readers will disagree with you. You bring up the point that in some capital cases, extenuating circumstances need to be considered more carefully. You cite the example of Karla Faye Tucker, the woman executed in Texas for a murder she committed 14 years earlier in a drug-induced frenzy. While in prison, she became a deeply religious person, committed to being a resource for others. Using supporting quotations from prison guards, religious leaders, and her victims' families would go a long way toward adding credibility to your emotional reaction.

You can even build an entire piece around a quotation. Anne Lamott in *Bird by Bird* writes that she organized an article about the Special Olympics around the quote, "Now that is one cool man." She had overheard a man with Down's Syndrome say this when he spotted himself in a photograph. Her article centered on how the Special Olympics helped build self-esteem, and the quotation was an effective tool for conveying this point (14: p. 42).

A startling remark in the introduction or conclusion is another way to use quotations. For example, if you're writing a paper on the harmful uses of nuclear power, you could begin like this: "Except for fools and madmen, everyone knows that nuclear war would be an unprecedented human catastrophe." That this is a quote by the famous scientist Carl Sagan makes the introduction or conclusion more forceful and credible.

Here are some guidelines for using quotations. 1) Include a phrase, such as "according to" or "so-and-so asserts," to indicate the source. If this phrase takes away from the quote's impact, at least give the source credit. For example, in the quotation about nuclear power, give credit to Carl Sagan somewhere in the paragraph, preferably just after the quote. 2) Rather than dropping the quotation into the prose, be sure that you explain its relevance to your point or topic. 3) Use quotations sparingly because too many of them can seem like substitutes for your own thoughts.

Anecdotes

Anecdotes are short scenarios or incidents told like a brief story to illustrate a point. When I was presenting type at a conference, I mentioned that intuitive thinking types (NTs) like to make their point by using definitions. Sometimes this trait can seem hair splitting, especially when used in legal scenarios, but I remember one time when it helped to ease tensions at our house.

When my son Dan was seven years old, he fell into the habit of whining and complaining when things didn't go his way. One day, when he was having an unusually bad time, his father said to him, "Quit skulking!" "What does 'skulking' mean?" asked Dan. His father, an NT, told him to get out the dictionary. When Dan looked up the definition, he turned to us with shock on his face: "It says 'Dan'!" We then turned to him with amusement on our faces: "'Dan' is an abbreviation for Danish. 'Skulk' is a Danish word, originating from the country of Denmark," we explained. This incident helped to lighten up both father and son.

Telling this anecdote helped my audience at the type conference better relate to the point about NTs and definitions. Anecdotes almost always enliven a speech or a piece of writing.

Figurative Language

Figurative language is useful when you want to make a point in a poetic or symbolic way. Some people shy away from figurative language because they don't know how to use symbols or imagery. But figurative language can make a point in a way that other techniques cannot, and it often paints a picture for the reader.

Figurative language usually uses comparisons to help make complex information more understandable. Here's an example of figurative language in the form of an analogy: "The phenomenon of electrons moving through a wire can best be understood by imagining a pipe completely filled with golf balls. If an additional ball is pushed in at one end of the pipe, a ball will pop out almost instantly at the other end. Similarly, when a distant power plant forces electrons into one end of a wire, other electrons almost immediately come out at the other end" (26: p. 219). An analogy uses something familiar, like golf balls, to help explain something unfamiliar, like the movement of electrons.

Computer and scientific concepts often need a central comparison such as an analogy to help the reader understand them. Comparing computer storage to a giant file cabinet takes the reader from the known (a file cabinet) into the unknown (computer storage).

Sometimes you may want to use figurative language to symbolize an experience or a feeling. In this case, you use a metaphor (a direct comparison) or a simile (using "like" or "as"). Perhaps you want to describe how you feel when you are tired by comparing yourself to an artificial plant. It looks lifeless and wilted rather than perky and full of energy. You feel like an artificial plant when you don't take time to nurture yourself. The plant stands as a symbol for something else — that is, the way you feel.

Metaphors and similes can also be used for vivid description. One of the most famous examples comes from *The Great Gatsby*, when F. Scott Fitzgerald describes his heroine's voice as "full of money." When using figurative language in descriptions, be careful that your comparisons aren't strained or cliched. "Her smile is as fresh as a daisy" is a cliche, but "her smile is as fresh as a daylily on a June morning" paints a picture with words.

Visuals

Visuals are another technique to use when direct language isn't enough. Used mostly in technical material, visuals either illustrate the most important points or guide the reader through the prose to make it more coherent. Here's a brief explanation of the most common visuals (26: pp. 188-207).

Tables: Tables usually illustrate the results of research. Writers use them to present numerical data so that readers can see the data quickly and in context. Tables are also used to compare numbers or features when there are many of them. Then, the need for a lengthy prose explanation can be eliminated.

TABLE

	ST	SF	NF	NT
ART/DRAMA	12	17	54	17
COACHING	37	34	14	15
ENGLISH	16	20	44	30
MATHEMATICS	35	28	13	24

**PERCENTAGE OF TEACHERS BY TYPE
IN DIFFERENT SPECIALTIES**

Line graphs: Line graphs can show trends, such as the population increase in your town over the last 50 years, annual profits or losses, or the percent return on investments with a particular company.

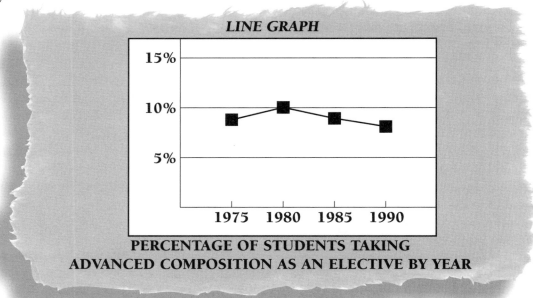

PERCENTAGE OF STUDENTS TAKING ADVANCED COMPOSITION AS AN ELECTIVE BY YEAR

Bar graphs: Bar graphs use rectangular bars to indicate the relative size of several variables. They can be used to compare similar units, such as population growth among two or three cities or countries, or to compare sizes or measure rates.

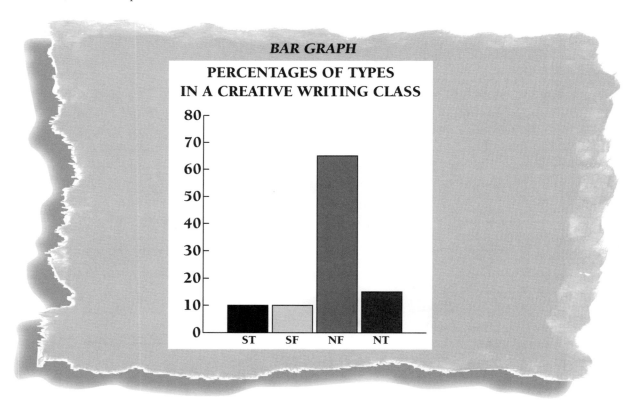

Write from the Start

Pie charts: Pie charts use circles to indicate percentages of a total, with the circle representing 100%. The pie-shaped segments represent each component's percentage of the total. They are best used to compare magnitudes that vary widely because they can't easily illustrate small differences in percentages. They compare components to one another and to the whole.

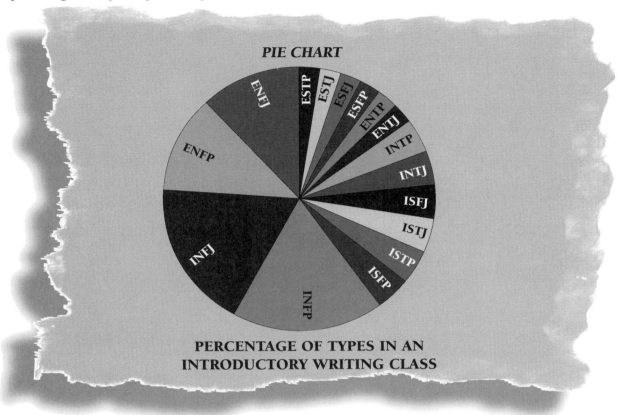

PIE CHART

PERCENTAGE OF TYPES IN AN INTRODUCTORY WRITING CLASS

Flow charts: Flow charts show a time or a decision sequence. They are used to help readers grasp a process. A decision chart is a kind of flow chart that explains whether or not to perform a certain action in a certain situation. At each point in the chart, the reader makes decisions about the progress of a project and then follows a path until the final goal is reached.

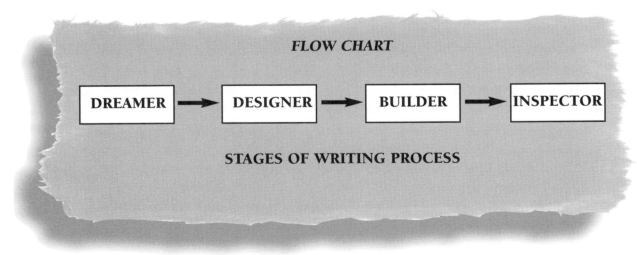

FLOW CHART

DREAMER → DESIGNER → BUILDER → INSPECTOR

STAGES OF WRITING PROCESS

Illustrations: Illustrations, such as maps, layouts, drawings, or photographs, are often used in sets of instructions and manuals. Illustrations show parts of an object clearly so that the reader can visualize the object. They are useful in eliminating unnecessary details in the prose so that the reader doesn't get bogged down and can focus on what is important.

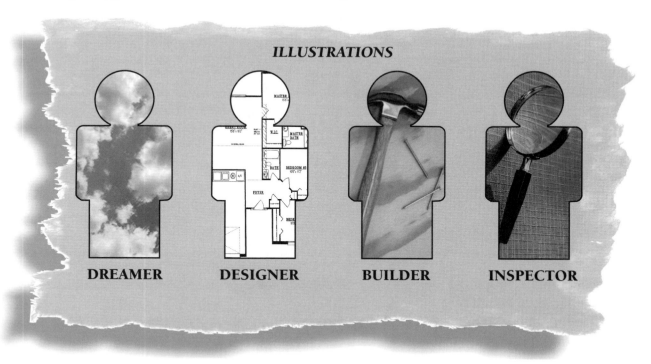

ILLUSTRATIONS

DREAMER   DESIGNER   BUILDER   INSPECTOR

The key to using visuals is to present them in a way that supplements and reports data honestly. They should never clutter the page or be used for show.

Developing content can make the difference between a substantive piece of writing and a weak one. Most of us gravitate toward familiar ways of developing our writing without trying those that would make our writing more forceful. And we often develop our content without considering the needs of our readers. Chapter Eight will show you how to draw on your less preferred processes (or nonpreferences) to consider a reader of another type and to build content.

For Practice:

1. Define an object or term that is not well known to most readers. You might choose an object that has parts, or a term that is abstract or vague.

2. Think of a person close to you and describe him or her without inserting how you feel. Describe physical appearance only, not personality characteristics.

3. Now describe this person using two examples of figurative language. (Her hair is as red as _____.) (His face reminded me of _____.)

4. Write a short anecdote as a lead into an article about how you have dealt with all the technological changes in the past ten years. (You might want to use some humor with this one.)

5. Think of a quotation from a famous person or something a friend recently said to you. How would you use it to develop your content or to add credibility?

Chapter Eight:

Using Your Nonpreferences in the Builder Stage

As you write your first drafts in the Dreamer and Designer Stages, you draw on your preferences. Relying on your preferences to start the paper will almost always break writer's block and reduce anxiety. However, in the Builder Stage, you are beginning to revise your paper. You can now allow your inner critic to emerge. He or she may have some useful things to say, such as "Why not take a risk and try some figurative language in paragraph three?" or "I know you don't like to use anecdotes because they seem too conversational, but an anecdote just might enliven paragraph four."

Since you're making more of an effort in this stage to relate to audience, you'll want to ask more specific questions. Use these three as a guideline.

1) What personality preferences will the readers likely have? For example, people in the business world usually prefer the thinking function whereas people in human services usually prefer the feeling function. Elementary teachers usually prefer sensing whereas college professors usually prefer intuition. Counselors and psychotherapists usually prefer intuition and feeling, while scientists often prefer intuition and thinking.

2) What is the purpose of the piece of writing? Perhaps you want to help an ESTJ manager make a decision that will affect the organization. You might want to persuade a rational INTJ physician to accept a mind-body program in his hospital. Maybe you want to explain to an ESFJ teacher why there isn't enough money for the materials she needs. Or perhaps you want to motivate an INFP minister to speak out on an unpopular issue. You need to consider whether the purpose of the piece is to inform, persuade, explain, or motivate.

3) What kind of document is it? Writing up minutes for a meeting and writing a psychology paper require different skills. Step-by-step instructions and philosophical essays will almost certainly need to be treated in two different ways. What is the best way to set up the piece so that the format fits the subject?

Since the functions (S/N and T/F) are more likely to affect content, I will focus on them rather than on E/I and J/P.

You'll begin by practicing with sensing and intuition, the opposite perceiving functions. Then you'll practice using thinking and feeling, the opposite judging functions.

All of us have characteristics of both sensing and intuition as well as thinking and feeling. At first, using the opposite function feels a little like writing with the non-dominant hand. But as we become more and more able to draw on all of our functions when we need to, we begin to move into wholeness.

Sensing and Intuition: Clarifying the Difference

If you're a sensing type, you probably like specific directions written simply and directly. You draw on your experience and like to cite verifiable material. You prefer to have as a model something that has worked before, whether it's a format for a report or a formula for a short story. You may use examples as illustrations of your point, or you may need examples from an author in order to grasp the concept. Sensing types value soundness of understanding.

If you are an intuitive type, you probably like to engage your imagination and create your own directions. You start with original ideas and write with subtlety or complexity. You like hypotheses and implications, and you may even try out new ways of writing a simple memo. Even if you neglect to put examples in your own writing, you like to see them in others' writing to help you grasp content quickly. You may even use the examples as a substitute for reading the entire report, especially instructions. Intuitive types value quickness of understanding.

Intuitive types are often deemed more creative than sensing types because they are more innovative, and "innovation" meets the popularly-held definition of "creative." Intuitive types are the ones who see connections and associations between seemingly disparate ideas or objects.

Sensing types have a different approach to creativity: they are "adaptors" rather than "innovators." They like to improve on something already existing, such as adapting new words to an old song. The outcome may not be a new insight but rather a very workable new product that stems from an old one.

The chart below briefly sums up the differences between the way sensing and intuitive types prefer to communicate.

Sensing Types:
- want and need specific, concrete detail for understanding
- focus on facts rather than theory
- seek reality-based, practical prose
- can report accurately on what is going on around them
- like to report on actual recalled experiences
- like to categorize and store sensory experiences for evaluating future experiences
- believe there is a "correct" way to write a document
- rely on "tried and true" models

Intuitive Types:
- can draw on a wide range of possibilities and options
- can perceive underlying and subtle aspects of a topic
- like to write about complex issues
- can generate a new angle on a topic
- like to use a varied vocabulary
- can experience a flow of images
- like to create their own model for writing

Since intuitive types tend to be more in touch with the unconscious mind and sensing types are more in touch with the physical world, their communication styles can differ greatly. Sensing types tend to hear communication literally, even if they don't take ideas literally. Intuitive types tend to talk in big picture terms and use abstract language.

Both sensing and intuitive types need to make a special effort to communicate with one another. However, it is up to intuitive types to communicate more clearly because if their word choice is vague or general, sensing types will not hear their message. The "leaps" that intuitive types sometimes make are not always apparent to a sensing type.

Because sensing types seem to outnumber intuitive types in the general population by as much as 3 to 1, most intuitive types will have to write for sensing type audiences at some point. And sensing types will often have to write for intuitive audiences in professional settings. Knowing how to write for different audiences can greatly boost a writer's confidence and lead to a more satisfying writing experience.

Write from the Start

Guidelines for Sensing Types

Let's say that a sensing type student is writing a paper for an intuitive type literature professor. The professor announces that students can earn a passing grade for a summary, but must have an original approach to earn an A or a B. The sensing student decides to take a risk and try to please the professor.

Here are some guidelines for tapping the intuitive function (after the student has written a first draft from the sensing preference).

- Develop a state of mind conducive to intuition. Consciously value intuition and intend to develop it by devoting time to it. Relax and let go of physical and emotional tension to give your intuition space.
- Cultivate a receptive attitude. Too much conscious programming or mental activity gets in the way of intuitive awareness. You may have to light a candle and sit in silence for 15 or 20 minutes. Listen to your inner guidance for inspiration.
- Engage in nonverbal play, such as drawing or music. Anything done in the spirit of play, rather than for goal-oriented achievement, provides a channel for flashes of insight.
- Accept and trust the process as it is unfolding. Intuition functions more freely with a non-judgmental attitude. Don't try to rush or force the intuitive process.
- Jot down your insights in a journal. This practice will validate your hunches so that you don't dismiss them (30: pp. 203-205).

These tips set the stage for awakening intuition so that it feels more natural when called for. Then when you're ready to write, try this step-by-step process.

1) Focus on the big picture. Do the parts fit together? Do the details, facts, and examples fit a theme? Sensing types like details, but may not see their implication.
2) Cluster to generate associations and connections that you might not have thought of in your first draft. Clustering will help you see new ideas and possibilities.
3) Look for a central image. Perhaps a metaphor would work. Ask: How is my topic like something else or something unfamiliar? (Example: One sensing type student used metaphor by comparing the experience of getting braces to going to jail. They both have bars, are confining, make you feel disgraced, etc....)
4) Look for the symbols connected to your topic. What do these symbols represent? For example, what does a parent represent to you beyond his or her role as Father or Mother? What does an animal say to you about your instinctual nature?
5) Find a quotation or a thought-provoking question that would take your piece beyond the literal and the obvious.

Now let's go through the writing process of a sensing type student who wanted to improve his piece by drawing on intuitive skills. The assignment was to bring an object from home to describe. The writer, an ISFP, began with a freewrite focusing on family relationships, earth-bound images, and vivid detail.

The Blue Rock

The blue rock is made of clay and sand, similar to a mixture to make bricks. It is a two-toned blue with the dark blue almost a black shadow cast in the concaved crevices of this hand-made rock. The surface is lumpy on top and flat on the bottom with several rough bubbly spots unevenly spread throughout. There are several areas where the blue paint has chipped off with 25 years of wear and tear, exposing the orange-red composition. On the bottom of the rock are the initials "TT" crudely engraved, the initials of my son Todd.

Todd made this rock as a gift for me in 1971 when he was three years old and attending a summer day camp. The initials were among the first he learned to write. Todd and I have always had a bond. We have built lasting memories and a relationship of trust and hope — a rock-solid bond. This rock also helps with the family as a whole. When I worry about family events, work, or everyday events in my life, Todd's rock is my worry stone.

This rock has served a utilitarian purpose in holding down items that otherwise might be pushed aside or fall behind the desk, lost and forgotten. Things of importance find their way under the rock for security and safekeeping. The rock has been a paper-weight at times in my office but more recently has occupied a prominent spot on my desk at home. It connects me to the earth and gives me a solid foundation. I can touch it, rub it, and find comfort in the stability it brings. It is cool, it is firm, and is an offering from my first-born; it is a gift that keeps on giving.

The writer revised his piece by bringing in symbolism and meaning. I encouraged him to cluster the rock; notice how the cluster brings in associations and imagery not included in the freewrite.

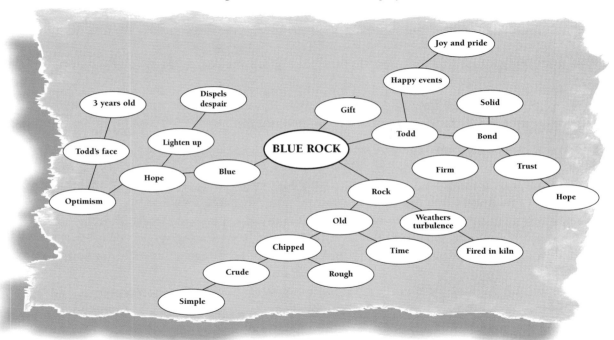

When the writer integrated his insight from the cluster into another draft, the piece became much richer. Notice how the changes make the draft more appealing to intuitive readers without losing its appeal to sensing readers.

The Blue Rock

The blue rock is made of clay and sand, similar to a mixture to make bricks. It is a two-toned blue with the dark blue almost a black shadow cast in the concaved crevices of this hand-made rock. The surface is lumpy on top and flat on the bottom with several rough bubbly spots unevenly spread throughout. There are several areas where the blue paint has chipped off with 25 years of wear and tear, exposing the orange-red composition. On the bottom of the rock are the initials "TT" crudely engraved, the initials of my son Todd. Todd made this rock as a gift for me in 1971 when he was three years old and attending a summer day camp. The initials were among the first he learned to write.

This rock has served a utilitarian purpose in holding down items that otherwise might be pushed aside or fall behind the desk, lost and forgotten. Things of importance find their way under the rock for security and safekeeping. For me, the important memories and relationship of trust and hope find lasting comfort under the care of our rock-solid bond.

The rock has been a paperweight at times in my office but more recently has occupied a prominent spot on my desk at home. It is more of a symbol reminding me of the lasting bond between Todd and me. Like a rock, we have a firm, lasting relationship that has weathered turbulence and shared the happy events in the passage of time. Often chipped and rough, we have continued to survive. For this crafted item to have survived, it had to be fired in a kiln or else it would have crumbled into grit and sand years ago.

Blue is a color of hope and optimism which I always retain even when there may be tension between Todd and me. This rock also helps me with the family as a whole. When I worry about family events, work, or everyday events in my life, Todd's rock is my worry stone. I can touch it, rub it, and find comfort in the stability it brings. The vision of a 3-year-old boy's face, and the joy and pride when he gave me this rock immediately diffuses the worry I face. This paperweight helps me to lighten up. It connects me to the earth and gives me solid foundation. I become grounded, and the sense of despair is dispelled. As simple and as crude as it is, it is cool, it is firm, and it is an offering from my first-born. It is a gift that keeps on giving.

If you are a sensing type, try one or two of these exercises to practice bringing intuitive qualities to your writing.

1. You have been asked to make a brief talk for your church service commemorating the anniversary of the Hiroshima bombing. The parishioners are mostly intuitive types. What symbols or images could you focus the talk around?
2. Look at a photograph you took on one of your vacations. Do a freewrite on a central image in the picture.
3. Think of someone who is very different from you and jot down his or her characteristics. What do you like or dislike about this person? How is this person a mirror of you?
4. Do a freewrite beginning with the word "imagine." It is okay to write an "imaginary scene" based on a true experience.

Guidelines for Intuitive Types

Now suppose that an intuitive type has to write for a sensing boss or teacher. Or suppose that the piece of writing is a technical report, a memo, or a set of instructions. How can intuitive types rework the first draft to make it more likely to satisfy their audience? First, intuitive writers need to tune into their senses.

- Sight: Draw or pay close attention to a color. Look around your room or office and notice patterns of color and design. Focus on details in a picture or piece of furniture. If you can go outside, notice the contrasts of colors and shapes in nature.
- Sound: Listen to sounds around you, such as the sound of a bird, a truck passing by, or a train whistle. Even focusing on the whirring of a machine can activate this sense.
- Taste: Notice the variety of flavors in your lunch. How do sweet and tart or hot and cold complement each other?
- Touch: Notice textures and contrasts. Contrast the softness of a pillow on your couch with the sharp edges of a paperweight on your desk.

- Smell: Be mindful of smells in the air. You might notice somebody's cologne or smells from the cafeteria. Step outside to smell the fragrance of the outdoors.
- Kinesthesia: Stretch, or simply walk down the hall or outside. Develop an awareness of your body in motion or at rest. Moving your body brings new ideas to mind.

Remember that the best writing is alive with sensation and that most readers need descriptive details. Try this step-by-step process to help build concrete details and practicality into your prose.

1) Cluster an abstract idea to generate details and examples. Relate these details to one or more of your senses.
2) Look for leaps between associations and connections in your cluster and tie them together.
3) Tie the theoretical into the real world of the tried and true, or what has worked before. You might think of an analogy that links your concept to the known; for example, how is a religious concept like something that is familiar in everyday life?
4) Look for the bottom line. State the main point up front and work down from it. Include background information, such as important dates presented in chronological order.
5) Spell out your ideas clearly. Too often, intuitive types write in such big-picture terms that sensing types can't find anything to get their hands on.

The assignment for this next writing sample was to describe an object from Guatemala: a small replica of a disabled "chicken bus" decorated with fruits and vegetables. A figure of a man is looking inside the hood. The writer, an ENFP, wrote a story, a natural way for an intuitive to start. She began by clustering the object to trigger ideas.

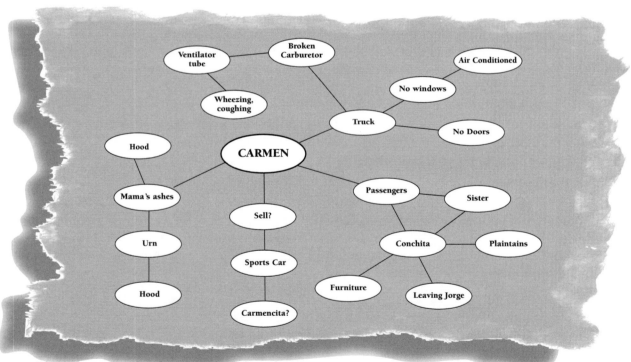

Then she wrote this freewrite from her cluster:

Carmen

My truck's name is Carmen. She has no windows or doors. I like her that way — air-conditioned. But Carmen has not been herself since my brother Juan Carlos took some gringos down to see the ruins of Tikal. Juan Carlos said there was a "little problem" with the carburetor which he fixed with a ventilator tube. One of the gringo doctors let him borrow the tube. But Carmen has been wheezing and coughing since we left Antigua, so I think she does not like the human ventilator tube.

Conchita is leaving her husband Jorge. This is the third time she has left Jorge. Each time she leaves, she moves everything out of the bar they own in Antigua and piles it on my truck. Conchita and her sister are crying and eating in the back seat.

When we reach her sister's house, we will pretend to unload the bus. Conchita and her sister will cry and eat more plantains, and we will listen for the telephone. In a short while, the phone will ring and it will be Conchita's husband calling to beg her to come back. Conchita will forgive him and we will drive everything back to Conchita's bar. We make money, so why not? Everyone is happy.

The trouble is, I cannot get the old hose to stay attached to the carburetor. May Santa Maria forgive me, but I used the urn with Mama's ashes to prop open the hood. I think maybe it is time to sell Carmen. Maybe I buy a sports car with only two seats. I will call her Carmencita.

I encouraged the writer to add sensory description to flesh out her piece. She looked again at the object and listed details.

yellow and blue truck	dishes	bushel of avocados
green racing stripe	chickens	basket of pomegranates
pig	barstool	plantains

When she wrote the next draft, the writer incorporated these details (and others from her imagination) to help the reader experience "being there" as she tells the story. The changes she made are underlined.

Carmen

My truck's name is Carmen. She has no windows or doors. I like her that way — air-conditioned. She is yellow and blue with a green racing stripe down the middle. But Carmen runs no races. She has not been herself since my brother Juan Carlos took some gringos down to see the ruins of Tikal. Juan Carlos said there was a "little problem" with the carburetor which he fixed with a ventilator tube. One of the gringo doctors let him borrow the tube. But Carmen has been wheezing and coughing since we left Antigua, so I think she does not like the human ventilator tube.

Conchita is leaving her husband Jorge. This is the third time she has left Jorge. Each time she leaves, she moves everything out of the bar they own in Antigua and piles it on my truck — the pig, the dishes, the chickens, and the barstool. She also takes all the food — a bushel of avocados, a basket of pomegranates, and many plantains. Conchita and her sister are crying and eating plantains in the back seat.

When we reach her sister's house, we will pretend to unload the plantains and chickens from the bus. Conchita and her sister will cry and eat more plantains, and we will listen for the telephone. In a short while, the phone will ring and it will be Conchita's husband calling to beg her to come back. Conchita will forgive him and we will drive everything back to Conchita's bar. We make four hundred pesos each way, so why not? Everyone is happy.

The trouble is, I cannot get the old hose to stay attached to the carburetor, and Conchita's chicken is eating the pomegranates on the top of the truck. The chicken hops on the hood which bangs my head like a castanet and gives me a headache worse than Jorge's homemade tequila. May Santa Maria forgive me, but I used the urn with Mama's ashes to prop open the hood.

Ay-yi-yi, that chicken is dancing the fandango on my head! I think maybe it is time to sell Carmen. Maybe I buy a sports car with only two seats, <u>one for me and one for the waitress in Conchita's bar. Yes, I buy a Mazda Miata, the color of jalapenos, the color of the waitress's lipstick.</u> I will call her Carmencita.

If you are an intuitive type, try one or two of these exercises for practice in tapping your sensing function:

1. Call a friend and make an effort to remember exactly what that friend said. Then jot down the conversation.
2. Read a paragraph from a book or magazine and take in as much detail as you can. Then jot down everything you remember.
3. Look at a picture in a travel magazine and list all the details in the picture.
4. Write a paragraph as part of a travel article to persuade your audience to visit a particular place. Appeal to as many senses as you can.

Even though sensing and intuition are opposite perceiving functions, a balance between the two is the ideal. People who rely almost exclusively on sensing to provide them with information might think that successful writing means following a formula or producing an error-free document. And people who rely almost exclusively on intuition might think that good writing means playing with ideas.

People with either preference need to experience their opposite preference before they can write from it. By looking beyond the literal, sensing types can learn to "read between the lines" and intuit meaning. And by observing life more closely and paying attention to people's exact wording (not just their overtones), intuitive types can learn to be more specific.

You will know when there is an interaction between sensing and intuition in your writing: facts will have more relevance, practical information will be presented in a more imaginative way, and stories will come alive with detail.

Thinking and Feeling: Clarifying the Difference

Some people score almost evenly on thinking and feeling when they take the MBTI. Believing that an even score is desirable, they say that they are equally adept at thinking and feeling and have no preference for one over the other. The truth is that they probably feel some conflict about thinking and feeling; this conflict usually stems from not understanding what thinking and feeling are about.

A common belief is that feeling types decide chiefly through their values. Actually, both types do, but thinking types may call their values "principles." The point is that feeling and thinking types value and evaluate differently. Thinking types make decisions (or evaluate) based on objectivity and fairness, while feeling types make decisions based on subjectivity and harmony.

A second belief is that thinking types can argue more effectively. While it is true that thinking types are more consistent about going from "point A to point B" and can stand back from the emotional side of an issue, feeling types can actually be more persuasive. Their ability to appeal to the heart can often sway the audience more readily than the thinking type's ability to appeal to the head.

A third belief about thinking and feeling concerns logic: the thinking type is adept at logic, and the feeling type isn't. Here, we are probably talking about logic in the traditional sense of the word — that is, logic as a form of reason, as in analysis or cause and effect.

However, feeling types may be just as logical in their own way. For example, consider this question from a survey about taking financial risk: Would you rather become wealthy by playing the stock market, or by inheriting a large sum? A financially conservative thinking type might reason that she would rather inherit a large sum because the stock market is too risky. Her answer would be the "logical" answer for someone in the low-risk category.

A feeling type might reason that he would rather play the stock market because inheriting money would mean that someone close to him would die. His answer would officially register in the high-risk category even though he may be a low-financial risk person. While his reasoning wouldn't lead to the "right" answer for his financial views, his logic is no more faulty than the thinking type's. The feeling type is using what we might call "logic of the heart."

Thinking and feeling types do write differently, and two of the most noticeable differences are in topic selection and audience awareness. Thinking type writers will likely decide on topics with some emotional distance rather than with personal involvement. They will focus on communicating clearly rather than on pleasing or relating to the audience. Here are some of the tendencies that thinking types bring to their writing.

- value clarity of thought
- like to work with cause-effect and analysis
- like to take a definite stand
- need for their arguments to "make sense"
- need to be consistent and complete in their argument
- like to search for "rational truth"
- are intense in their arguments
- like to work with problem-solution
- may not notice tone
- strive for precise language for clarity
- like to build frameworks and fit facts into that framework
- like question-answer format
- like to use definitions to clarify

How can thinking types revise (in the Builder Stage) when they have to write on a subjective topic or for a feeling audience?

Guidelines for Thinking Types

- Try to personalize the situation. If the topic is capital punishment, imagine that the criminal is a member of your family.
- Use persuasion as well as argument. That is, get away from facts and statistics to convince and make an emotional appeal. Ask your audience: How would you feel if a child abuser were released from prison in a year and moved into your neighborhood?
- Interview or write a dialogue with a feeling type to generate ideas for writing on a subjective topic. Ask: What are the feeling values here? Why is harmony so important? How will group harmony contribute to a more effective solution or outcome? Why do I need to be tactful anyway?
- Get away from the overriding issue of fairness and ask this question: "What matters most to me and to the people affected by my decision?"
- Cluster a feeling, perhaps "anger" if you are writing about an emotional issue (such as child abuse).
- Write another draft without regard to structure; allow yourself to follow the flow of your thoughts.
- Try a personal example or an anecdote. These tend to get you out of your head.
- Have something visual in front of you to remind yourself of your audience, such as a picture of a friend or loved one. After each paragraph, ask: How will "my" audience react to this message?

- If the piece is controversial, organize the topic around problem-solution rather than around argumentation. Then concentrate on offering a solution that is in the best interest of your audience.
- Appeal to the more "human" side of your audience. This doesn't mean you have to be sentimental or emotional.

Here's an example of why it might be important to write more subjectively when you are trying to persuade your audience.

Last year, our neighborhood lake began to turn the color of red clay due to sediment and run-off from the construction of nearby housing projects. Several neighbors held a meeting and decided to seek legal action. The challenge was to rally more people behind this cause so that we could raise money for the legal fees. Since three of the neighbors were scientists, they compiled statistics and facts from studies done on the lake to convince others to join the fight. They wrote this letter.

Dear Homeowners:

At our first meeting with the county's Erosion Control Officers, we were informed that the turbidity levels in our lake were to be expected given the amount of construction upstream. We were also told that the turbidity levels would remain high for between two to five years and that we should expect the turbidity to get worse. The turbidity levels have gone from 13 a year ago to 500 this year.

The Erosion Control Officers have dismissed our concerns, noting the lake cleared up for a period over the summer. The lake even cleared to the point that some residents began to swim and fish. However, the lake's clarity was not due to improvements in construction practices upstream, but was due to the lack of rainfall. With one good rain, the lake became muddy again.

Having exhausted every remedy without effect, the Homeowners Board has decided to sue three of the five upstream developers for the damage they have caused to the lake. We have retained the services of an environmental law firm. Our lawyers believe we have ample evidence and legal standing to sue.

We ask for contributions from all homeowners to help with legal fees. We believe that we have a good case and certainly a good cause. Please see attachment for particulars of the case, including our law firm, our attorney, and the distribution of monies. We will let you know when to send a check, and thank you for your commitment.

Money for the cause began to trickle in, but it took several follow-up letters and arm-twisting to spur action. The concerned scientists then decided to write a series of articles in the neighborhood newsletter telling why the lake was important to them. Here's one of the articles, written by an INTJ.

Critters

One of my greatest pleasures is sitting out on my deck in the early morning, reading the paper, having my first cup of coffee, and listening to the various critters that share our lake and its environs. The lake and surrounding land provide several ecosystems where a host of animals can live. We see some, but many are only evident by the sounds they make.

The deep chug-o-rums of the bullfrogs, which can reach a foot or more in length, are comforting sounds from my youth in rural New Jersey. Another lake resident is the half-inch-long southern cricket frogs that live in the marshy area below the spillway. Just stand there awhile and listen: you'll first hear one or two tentative notes which soon turn into a chorus of raspy clicks sounding something like those little metal party clickers. It's amazing how such a big sound can come from such a small source — a source we'll likely never see.

My wife, Ann, and I have mentioned now and again how much fun it would be to sleep out on our deck sometime and enjoy the sounds of our wild neighbors (no, not Paul, Blair, Al, Karen, or Kathy). Anyway, one night we moved to the basement apartment which has a ground level window, opened the window wide, and went to bed. The night was alive with sound — crickets, katydids, frogs, toads, and who knows what else. We were still awake at midnight!

About that time, a family of barred owls began hooting outside our window, and a raccoon came by making its distinctive trilling call. It almost seemed that the owls and raccoon were now sitting outside our window looking in. At that point, we decided enough was enough, closed the window, and finally got to sleep.

We all have wild neighbors we do not know, and getting to know them better can be part of the satisfaction of living near our lake.

The series of articles that appeared in the newsletter accomplished what the objective business letters had not: the neighbors began to think about what the lake meant to them, and more money soon followed.

For thinking types who are mainly concerned with "getting the job done," writing that needs to be more personal may suffer. If you are a thinking type, try one or two of these exercises to help you relate to audience and build goodwill:

1. Think of a trait you value, such as competency or being responsible, and write a letter thanking a business or an organization for a job well done.

2. Imagine that you are a thinking type marriage counselor. You are in the middle of a session when the wife suddenly bursts into tears. The husband gets angry and starts criticizing her. As an exercise, you suggest that they write a letter to one another. How do you guide them in their use of language?

3. You are a thinking type boss who has to fire a feeling type employee. Write a memo asking the employee to meet you in your office to discuss his or her work.

4. You are a thinking type employee who must correct a feeling type boss in a meeting. How would you phrase your correction?

Unlike thinking types, feeling types are often acutely attuned to their audience and will usually try to relate to them. They gravitate toward topics in which they have some personal investment. Here are some of the tendencies that feeling types might follow in their writing.

• consider audience reaction above all else
• like to write about relationships
• have a clear sense of what is appropriate
• like a friendly tone
• need to write about their feelings for clarity on an issue
• like to use emotional appeals to persuade
• like to write about their personal values and traditions
• like to write to gain peace of mind about an upsetting issue
• like to express themselves through poetry
• use precise language to capture their feeling "tone"
• exclude or ignore what they don't like
• avoid taking a clear stand on a controversial topic

So how can a feeling type revise when faced with a dry, dispassionate topic or a thinking type audience? Here are some suggestions to use in the Builder Stage.

Guidelines for Feeling Types

- Explain the issue without making reference to its effect on yourself.
- Pose some hard questions and refrain from easy answers. Approach the questions objectively without sentiment or idealism.
- List or jot down objective information, such as facts and statistics, to back up your argument. For example, in arguing for gun control, consider how many gun-related deaths occurred over the past year. Find out how other countries have successfully banned handguns.
- Cluster an opposing viewpoint and write quickly without weighing your associations against your feelings.
- Write an active imagination dialogue with a thinking type that you are close to. Let the answers come from that person instead of from you.
- If the piece is controversial, organize around cause and effect. This pattern feels less opinionated than taking a strong stand.
- Think of the audience as non-judgmental. If you think you won't be attacked, you are more likely to speak your mind.
- Write a clear statement and work down from it rather than dancing around the issue or simply following the flow of your thoughts.
- Look for "non sequiturs" or places where the reasoning process doesn't follow.
- Write a definition to clarify a term.
- Include a visual to help guide your readers logically through the prose.

Feeling types' writing often reflects idealism and harmony, but sometimes they have to stand back and be objective. If they do not, a thinking type audience may dismiss their writing as overly sentimental or even unrealistic. Writing about emotion-filled topics in an objective way can help feeling types gain some perspective on their emotions and relate better to thinking types. I often suggest posing a question using the word "why" to help feeling types analyze their writing from a more objective point of view. Asking "why" helps to tap the thinking function.

One INFP writer decided to submit an article to the local newspaper on Christmas stress. After writing a first draft on his ideal Christmas, he clustered the question "Why is Christmas stressful?"

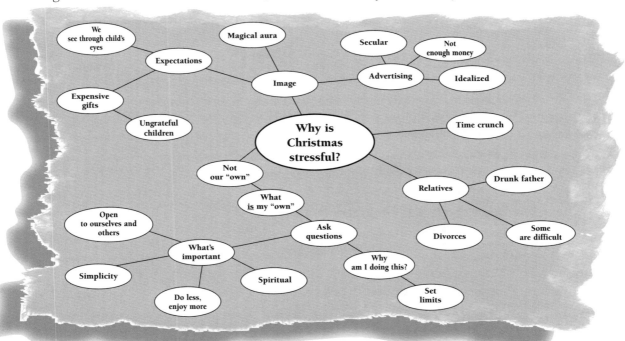

This writer's first draft was filled with images that portray Christmas as a time of hope, joy, perfect presents, and ideal relationships. When he incorporated the material from his cluster into his final draft, the result was a more balanced piece. He could then help his audience cope with the holiday season in a more realistic way. Here's an excerpt from his article (which was not only accepted by the newspaper but was also well received by the readers).

Reducing Holiday Stress

Television and magazine advertisements present an ideal image of a family Christmas with warm fires, beautiful gifts, food for a feast, grateful children, and rested families happy to be together.

Few, if any, holiday celebrations can live up to that ideal picture. We may be excited to see some of our relatives, but not all of them. The food that looks so good in full-color photographs leaves us feeling gorged and guilty and less competent as cooks. We may have moments of peace, love, and joy, but we're also stressed-out, exhausted, and ready for some quiet time.

Our ideal Christmas is never stressful, but the real Christmas often is. Why? Because many of us are trying to celebrate someone else's Christmas.

We may be trying to celebrate the Christmas that our spouses, children, and other relatives want, believing that somehow we must do it all. We may be trying to celebrate the Christmas we remember as a child, the magical Christmas that seemed to appear without effort and fill us with joy. Or we may be trying to celebrate the Christmas we wish we'd had if our family had had more money, or if our parents hadn't divorced, or if our Dad hadn't been drunk.

What can we do to make our celebrations of Christmas "our own" and not "someone else's"?

We can take some time to ask ourselves: What makes Christmas special for me? What is most important to me? What do I do just because I think I should, or because I'm trying to please or impress someone else? Make a list of all the holiday tasks you actually do, and decide which ones you can simplify, give up, or get help with. Keep asking yourself, "Is this important?" and "What's the worst thing that will happen if I don't do this?" and "Am I doing more than my share?"

Especially when we're trying to fulfill old childhood fantasies or the expectations of others, we may feel we can't say no or set limits. We often overlook the personal cost of not setting limits on what we will do. But with practice and encouragement, we can. Simplifying our holiday celebration may mean doing less in order to enjoy and appreciate more.

Whatever changes we make in how we observe the holidays, we will surely feel it was worth the effort if we are able to open up a little more with those we love and to a deeper part of ourselves.

If you are a feeling type, try one or two of these exercises for practice in tapping your thinking function:

1. You are a child psychologist. The parents are having differences of opinion over spanking. You are against spanking, but the child is clearly out of control and they have tried everything. Write out some guidelines for them, including the possibility of spanking.
2. You are a consultant giving writing workshops for Marines. They would rather "fight than write." What language would you use to motivate them?

3. Think of a tradition or holiday that involves getting together with extended family. You feel that the celebration has lost some of its meaning and you would like to change some of the rituals. Write a family letter explaining your unhappiness and outlining the changes you hope for.

4. You have been invited to speak before a group of thinking type business people on "How to Reduce Negativity in the Workplace." This particular group has a reputation for being negative. What approaches would you use in your talk?

Some unfortunate misunderstandings can arise between thinking and feeling types. Thinking types may think that feeling types are hopelessly sentimental, touchy-feely, or fuzzy-headed, while feeling types may feel that thinking types are hopelessly blunt and uncaring. These misunderstandings are precisely why both types have to watch their language and their tone when communicating with one another. Feeling types can learn to write more objectively about sentimental topics, and thinking types can blend their analytical reasoning with care and compassion.

Having a clear sense of audience and purpose helps you to flesh out your writing. Learning to use your less preferred functions in the Builder Stage adds to your natural writing skills so that you can relate to your audience and address your purpose more effectively.

Turning now to the Inspector, let's look at some ways to draw on both our preferences and non-preferences when editing the final draft.

Chapter Nine: The Inspector

After the house is built comes the walk-through. You go through each room inspecting the details. Do the outlets work? Is the wiring faulty? Do the seams in the wallpaper come together? Are the windows and doors properly sealed? Without tending to these details, you probably wouldn't feel secure living in the house.

You go through much the same process in the Inspector Stage as you "walk through" your piece of writing. Are the sentences in a logical order within paragraphs? Are the words in the most effective order within sentences? Do your words express exactly what you want to say? Are there typographical and spelling errors? Without this kind of scrutiny, your piece is incomplete.

As you look at the words under the Inspector column, think of the inspector's purpose. Can you think of any other words to add?

Dreamer	Designer	Builder	Inspector
whimsical	big picture	construct	refine
creative	form	add to	details
playful	organize	flesh out	scrutinize
imaginative	order	develop	cut down
child-like	layout	make	critique
full of wonder	framework	put together	take apart
chaotic	theme	erect	move around
free	pattern	carve	polish

One key word is "refine." Refining isn't the same as merely revising or editing. Even if you revise much of your work as you go along, you'll find in the Inspector Stage that you need to refine your piece even further. The inspector techniques outlined in this chapter will help you scrutinize and critique your work so that it sounds smooth and polished. You'll find tips for writing coherent paragraphs, crafting effective sentences, selecting the best word to express meaning, and proofreading for errors.

If you find that you need more help with grammar and mechanics, check the appendix. The sentence patterns should help with punctuation. The list of resources includes computer software programs that help with such grammar points as modifiers and pronouns as well as general readability and style. And, of course, most everyone knows about spell-check by now.

Another option is to show your work to an English whiz friend. I like to show my work to other English "experts" because I know how difficult it is to see my own writing with fresh eyes. For example, I had three different people "inspect" near-final drafts of this workbook. However you approach the last stage of the writing process, the key is to pay attention to those details that refine and polish the finished product.

Techniques for the Inspector Stage

All types can benefit from the techniques in this chapter. The exercises are sprinkled throughout the chapter rather than placed at the end so that you can determine your comfort level as you go. My suggestion is for you to try any of the exercises as needed.

Paragraphs

In the Designer Stage, you organized your main thoughts into units of ideas. These units of ideas, called paragraphs in the Inspector Stage, usually range from three to eight sentences revolving around one main idea. If your main idea results in more material than eight sentences can handle, it is better to write several shorter paragraphs than to write one long one. Long paragraphs swamp ideas and overwhelm the reader, while short paragraphs highlight the main idea and psychologically motivate the reader. I use the word "psychologically" here because white space on a page conveys the feeling of a break, like taking a breath. Also, you have a sense of accomplishment when you come to the end of a paragraph, especially if you've understood it!

In the Builder Stage, you developed your paragraphs with facts, descriptions, definitions, concrete examples, figurative language, anecdotes, quotations, and visuals. This development of the main idea is crucial for the reader to understand your message. Intuitive types, as you have seen, might not help sensing types understand their abstractions if they aren't made specific by an illustration or example. By this time in the writing process, your paragraphs should be developed well enough so that the reader comes away with a clear message of what you're trying to communicate.

Paragraphs aren't complete, though, until they're unified. This unity comes about by arranging your sentences skillfully within the paragraph. Most writers begin with some kind of statement of purpose, sometimes called a topic sentence and sometimes called a "power" or "umbrella" statement. Whatever you call it, be sure that all the other sentences relate to it and are arranged in some kind of logical order.

For example, you might go from general to specific, starting with a sentence like this: "It is time for our office to buy a new copier." The next sentence might read, "Our old copier continues to jam, resulting in wasted time, money, and paper." Perhaps in the next sentence you would mention how many times the copier jammed over the last month and how much money it would cost to repair it. What information would logically come next? How would you proceed through the paragraph to get to the most specific information?

In this paragraph pattern, sometimes called a "subordinate" pattern, all of the information springs from the main idea and becomes increasingly more detailed. The subordinate pattern can best be illustrated by an inverted pyramid (A).

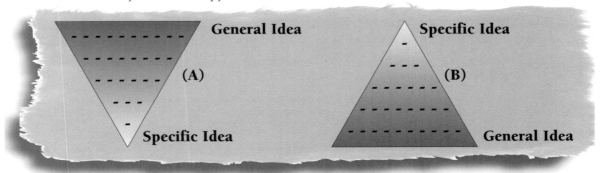

Sometimes a subordinate paragraph begins with the most specific information, which becomes increasingly general until it reaches the topic sentence. It may best be illustrated by an upright pyramid (B).

As you read the paragraph below, notice how the information begins with the most specific information and leads to the topic sentence.

The Mexican holiday "El Grito de Delores" stems from an event that happened on September 16, 1810. A priest named Miguel Hidalgo gathered his parishioners at his church in Dolores, Guanajuato, Mexico, to urge them to fight for freedom from Spain. Every year, the people of Mexico gather in the main plaza of their towns to shoot fireworks and wave Mexican flags. Although the Mexican people may feel divided over politics at other times of the year, "El Grito de Delores" unites them. It is one of the most important holidays in all of Mexico (Adapted — 17: pp. 217-218).

In the subordinate pattern, sentence order is important because order provides a sense of flow of information within the paragraph. At other times, the sentences convey equally important information. This pattern is called "coordinate" because the paragraph brings together, or coordinates, like and equal information. Block lists and step-by-step instructions are often written as a coordinate paragraph. Its form can best be illustrated by a square.

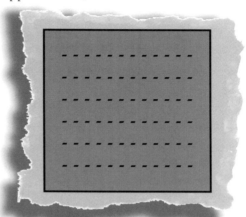

Here's an example of a coordinate pattern.

Our copier is exhibiting the following problems:
1) It consistently jams the paper.
2) It skips pages during collation.
3) It fails to process the toner adequately.
4) It cuts off during the warm-up phase.
5) It can no longer print on both sides of the paper.

In this pattern, you are not trying to convince the reader that one problem is more serious than another one; you are simply listing the problems. Also, the sentences aren't necessarily arranged in a logical or sequential order.

Now try writing two coordinate paragraphs. Here are possible topic sentences to get you started. "Living in a townhouse in a large city offers a number of advantages." "On the other hand, living in an old farm house in the country offers advantages, too."

When you look over your sentences in both subordinate and coordinate paragraphs, ask yourself these questions: Are the sentences understandable? Are they easy to follow? If the answer is "no" or even a reserved "yes," they are probably not coherent to the reader. Coherency means able to be understood in one reading. Three basic techniques help increase paragraph coherency: 1) transitions, 2) key words, and 3) definitions.

1) Transitions are like road signs that point the way for your reader. They help you move from one sentence to the next, or even to the next paragraph. If you want to introduce an illustration, you might use "for example," "for instance," or "to illustrate." If you want to add information, use "furthermore," "also," or "in addition." To point out a contrast, begin your sentence with "however," "on the other hand," or "nevertheless." To indicate a result, begin with "therefore," "hence," or "consequently." For time relationships, write "recently," "afterwards," or "in the meantime."

The paragraph below contains several transitions. Which ones do you recognize?

Red-tape has increased at our HMO over the last two years. For example, last year our HMO required us to fill out one form before we could get a referral. Now we have to fill out three forms for the same referral. Our HMO asks that we make our appointments by phone instead of in person at the desk, even if we are on the premises. Last week, I spent twenty minutes just making my annual appointments. This amount of time didn't include the five minutes it took to push all the buttons just to get the right department. Despite the inconvenience of the paperwork and extra phone time, though, I'm grateful for the quality care our HMO provides.

Sentence Pattern #5 in the appendix suggests more transitions. By becoming more aware of them, you can learn to use transitions more naturally and effectively.

2) Repeating key words is also important for coherence. For example, in the paragraph you just read, a key word is "HMO." If the writer had switched to "our health plan" or had written the name of the HMO, the reader might be confused. Also, if the writer had switched from "we" to "patients," the reader would have to work harder to understand the paragraph.

Now try writing a work or school-related paragraph repeating key terms. Here are some possible topic sentences:

"My boss is more demanding than he was a year ago." "One of my co-workers is starting to get on my nerves." "My job responsibilities have increased over the past year." "This semester is the most diffi-cult one yet."

Paragraph

_____

_____

_____

_____

_____

_____

_____

_____

_____

_____

3) Definitions, especially relating to jargon terms and acronyms, are another way to ensure para-graph coherency. If your audience understands the computer terms "baud" and "byte," then you won't have to define these terms. However, some audiences don't know that "baud" means the speed of the modem; in fact, they might not know exactly what the modem is! Better to explain than assume. How many terms do you understand in the following paragraph?

A valve actuator is a device that allows the hydraulic system's pressure to regulate the flow of the system. As oil enters the inlet port of this actuator, a pressure builds up. When this pressure exceeds the preset value, the rod extends. A cam, which is mounted on the rod, delivers the work. It then comes in contact with the desired valve to be opened or closed (26: p. 220).

Write from the Start

Did you have to look up terms? If you guessed at their meanings, are you sure you guessed them accurately? Here's a list of the terms you probably didn't know: valve actuator, hydraulic system, inlet port, preset value, cam. How could the writer have helped you understand these?

Now list five jargon words that you use on the job, or in some other area of your life. Then define any words that a lay reader probably wouldn't understand.

1. _____

2. _____

3. _____

4. _____

5. _____

Effective Sentences

Sentences are like the pictures you choose to express yourself in each room of your house. They are the colors that make a room come alive; they are the furniture placed in just the right way; they are the fabrics that blend and match. A paragraph made up of well-written sentences will invite the reader to sit down, linger, enjoy, and be enchanted by the prose you have created. Regardless of whether you are writing a letter or a novel, the reader must be engaged — and it is through the crafting of effective sentences that readers are lost or won.

In business writing, efficiency characterizes effective sentences. For memos and reports, you are writing to inform or perhaps to persuade, not to entertain or inspire. Your job is to communicate in short, easy-to-understand sentences so that the reader doesn't have to read the document twice to grasp it. Still, you don't want to bore your reader by writing choppy sentences of all the same type.

Variety is one key to successful sentences. The sentence patterns in the appendix show you how to write a variety of sentences. Turn now to the appendix on page 127 for a close look at these sentence patterns. Then, in the space below, try your hand at composing an example of each pattern.

1. _____
   _____

2. _____
   _____

3. _____
   _____

4. _____
   _____

5. _____
   _____

6. _____

_____

7. _____

_____

8. _____

_____

9. _____

_____

Pay particular attention to sentence patterns #6 and #7 when you're striving for variety. These sentence patterns not only add a level of sophistication to your writing, but they also provide opportunities for writing more interesting sentences.

For example, consider these two sentences: "Even though he tried hard, he couldn't scale the wall." "Try as he might, he couldn't scale the wall." The second sentence has more impact because "try as he might" reverses the usual word order of subject-verb-complement. It is also more direct as it moves the reader more quickly into the main thought of the sentence.

Instead of "When I get home, you and I must talk," try writing "As soon as I get home, you and I must talk." The meaning of the second sentence is more precise because "as soon as" creates more of a sense of urgency or immediacy than "when."

Instead of "Since I have finished my classes, I have more time," try writing "Now that I have finished my classes, I have more time." Does "since" in the first sentence express time or reason? "Now that" in the second sentence gives a clearer sense of the time relationship probably intended in the first sentence.

Pruning needless words and phrases is also crucial to writing effective sentences. Wordiness obstructs the flow that guides readers along. To help you to write more concisely and to improve your style, use this checklist.

Five Quick Ways to Improve Your Style

1. Underline all forms of the verb "to be" (be, am, is, are, was, were, been, being). Ask yourself if you can substitute an action verb or if you can edit out the "be" verb altogether.
2. Underline each "and" in your piece. Now look for other ways to combine the ideas.
3. Underline each "of" in your piece. Are they all necessary, or do they simply lead to wordiness?
4. Examine each word containing three or more syllables. Can you use a one- or two-syllable word instead?
5. If your sentences average over twenty words, look for ways to shorten them. Or consider making two sentences.

Point #1, substituting active verbs for "be" verbs, can go a long way toward enlivening your prose. Compare these two sentences: 1) The teacher's lecture was on the differences between Earth rocks and Mars rocks. 2) The teacher discussed the differences between Earth rocks and Mars rocks. When "was" in the first version becomes "discussed" in the revised version, the teacher stands up and does something.

Editing out the "be" verb often edits out the passive voice. Consider this sentence: "The report was written by the committee." The active form of the verb (wrote) is buried in the phrase "was written," and the subject (committee) is buried in a prepositional phrase. Better to write the sentence in the active voice: "The committee wrote the report." It's shorter and more direct.

Write from the Start

For practice with active verbs, write five sentences using the verbs below, avoiding any form of the verb "be." Notice how forceful and strong your sentences sound.

express	describe	appraise	solve	transform
distinguish	evaluate	produce	select	classify

1. _____

_____

2. _____

_____

3. _____

_____

4. _____

_____

5. _____

_____

Look in the appendix on page 131 for a list of other active verbs to refer to when your sentences need to stand up and do something.

After you've taken your sentences through the "Five Quick Ways to Improve Your Style" checklist, go back through and ask this question: Do all my words and phrases contribute to meaning? If not, edit them out. Be particularly alert for phrases starting with the word "that." Many times these phrases can be changed to one word or left out altogether.

Example: "The books that you need for the class are on the table." This sentence can be changed to "The books for the class are on the table." Another example: "The breath that you take in relaxes you and connects mind and body." How about: "Breathing techniques relax you and connect mind and body." Always ask yourself if you can shorten the sentence without destroying its essence.

Parallelism is another technique to improve sentence flow. In writing, parallelism means balancing the parts of the sentence grammatically. Here's an example: "Jane enjoys playing tennis, walking in nature, and exercising at the gym." The three activities that Jane enjoys all end with ing words, making them parallel.

How is the following sentence unparallel and wordy? "By purchasing this equipment, we would cut down on errors, and expenses in the long run would be reduced."

Here's a possible solution: "By purchasing this equipment, we would reduce errors and expenses." How many words have been cut? What part of the sentence uses parallelism?

Parallelism is particularly useful for setting up lists and putting items in a series. It helps make the sentence clear and less wordy. For practice, use parallelism in these lists and sentences. Start by picking out the item or the part of the sentence that is unparallel.

1. I would like to learn the following from this chapter:
   • How to start editing
   • Punctuation
   • How to develop paragraphs

2. Please observe the following rules for this class:
    - Rough drafts must be written two weeks ahead.
    - You must show your rough draft to the professor.
    - Final drafts must be turned in on time.
3. Here are three methods for improving coherency:
    - transitions
    - repeating key words
    - defining jargon terms
4. The professor explained the student's grade frankly, clearly, and with sympathy.
5. Presenting the material clearly is as important as to collect accurate information.

By using the "Five Quick Ways to Improve Your Style" checklist and employing parallelism, work with these next sentences to give them more life, to make them clearer, and to cut out wordiness.

1. We recommend that spouses be invited and in the case of single employees that they be allowed to bring one guest.
2. As a result of the increase in membership, your dues are going down.
3. Morgan Enterprises uses that system and saves its customers 20 percent.
4. The tennis camps at Hilton Head are ranked among the top 100 camps in the world by leading tennis magazines.
5. At the local university last spring, a sophomore was accused of plagiarizing papers from the Internet by a senior.

Word Choice

Why is using the right word important? The right word produces an image in the reader's mind. In a tennis game, one player might say that the ball "hit" the line. Another might say the ball "grazed" the line. What is the difference between the mental picture of the ball "hitting" the line and "grazing" the line? When you're trying to come up with just the right word for the image, consider these points.

1) If the word isn't exactly right, it must be exactly wrong. Never use a word that "will do"; the English language is infinitely varied and colorful.
    How does word choice change your mental image in these two sets of sentences? (a.) "Sam walked into the room." "Sam sauntered into the room." (b.) "We are working on the project." "We are collaborating on the project."

2) There are no such things as perfect synonyms. If two words conveyed exactly the same meaning, one of them (usually the harder to pronounce) would have dropped from the language from lack of use. Do the words "smart" and "intelligent" convey the same meaning? How about "since" and "because"? "Glum" and "gloomy"? Why not?

3) Think of your writing as a painting. Words are the hues of your colors; how you mix the words on the palette of your sentences determines the cast of the paragraphs. What would Monet's "Waterlilies" be like if he hadn't taken the time to create delicate pastels, rationalizing that the brighter tones were okay all by themselves?

In *The Writer's Art*, James Kilpatrick stresses the importance of the right mix of words. To illustrate, he cites this passage, written by the journalist Shana Alexander: "Patty Hearst is a Madonna dolorosa, a classic image of female suffering. She sits motionlessly, and tears fall from her eyes as from a Sicilian painting. Fine-featured, smooth-skinned, narrow, and pale, she is almost as white as the 'Pieta' of Michelangelo" (13: p. 46).

4) "They'll know what I mean" is a cop-out. The only person who really knows what you mean is you. Meaning is as much implicit as it is explicit; the implicit meaning of your words (their connotation) conveys as much as the words themselves.

   Do "home" and "house" imply different things? How about "man" and "gentleman"? "Dog" and "mutt"? "Religious" and "spiritual"?

5) Be obsessive, but not compulsive. That is, make a commitment to having your words say what you mean, but don't feel compelled to spend hours composing everything you write. Use the importance of what you're saying as a measure for your diligence.

For example, if you're writing a memo to announce a new procedure, you may not need to select your words as carefully as you would if you're trying to relay a more esoteric or technical idea. If the procedure you're announcing is controversial, though, you do need to think about the effect of your words to avoid insulting or intimidating someone. The tone of your piece plays an important role in successful communication.

Tone conveys your attitude toward your message and your reader. The words you choose convey your tone. For example, if your tone is informal, you'll probably use more contractions and personal pronouns, such as "you" and "I." If your tone is formal, you'll tend to use words like "furthermore" and "consequently." If your tone needs to convey goodwill, you'll want to use words like "appreciate" and "thank you."

Analyze these two sentences for tone: 1) "In your letter, you claim that the item was already broken when it arrived." 2) "In your letter, you state that the item was already broken when it arrived." The first sentence implies doubt that the item was already broken. The tone borders on being accusatory because of the word "claim."

Suppose you're in charge of collecting past-due accounts for a large department store. One customer has always paid his bill on time, but for the last two months, there has been no word from him. You believe he is a reliable person, but he has gotten into trouble with his debts. One of your colleagues writes a letter to him that begins like this: "For the second month in a row, you have failed to pay your balance due. Surely by now you have had time to let us know why we have not heard from you."

Which word in the first sentence would make the customer feel negative about paying his bill? Which word in the second sentence sounds sarcastic? How would you start a letter to the customer that would accomplish your purpose of collecting on the past-due account?

As you read the letter below, underline the words that suggest a negative tone.

Dear Mrs. Brown:

   This letter is to inform you that your appeal for your deceased husband's insurance is denied because you neglected to pay your premium within the grace period. Therefore, your policy expired just before your husband did.

   I know this is a hardship for you and your eight children, but rules are rules. It's unfortunate that you didn't pay attention to the "date due" portion of your insurance bill. We hope you will be more responsible in the future.

Sincerely,

Ima Taskmaster

What do the words in this letter say about the writer? What words would you change to ensure a positive response?

Mark Twain once said, "A powerful agent is the right word. Whenever we come upon one of those intensely right words, the resulting effect is physical and spiritual, and electrically prompt."

Stay alert to "right words." Whenever you come across one in your reading, underline it or write it down in a journal and then use it in your writing. The right word helps give your writing a voice.

Proofreading

Spotting typographical and spelling errors is harder for some people than for others. If this skill is difficult for you, you might try putting a sheet of paper under each line so that you see individual words and sentences rather than whole paragraphs. Looking at the separate parts helps you more readily detect errors. You might also try reading a sentence backwards to help you see what you might have missed.

For wordiness, you might pretend that you have to reduce a page and a half of information to one page. Look for parts of each sentence that can be shortened or cut until you get it all on one page. Although challenging, this exercise is enlightening because we often think we need all the words we've written.

For the essential mechanical and grammatical points, ask:

- Are commas and other punctuation marks in place? Ask a friend for help or use one of the resources in the appendix.

- Are apostrophes included where needed? Look for words that end in "s." Then ask yourself whether the word is plural or whether it is showing ownership. Watch out for the apostrophe in "it's." Don't use it unless you mean "it is."

- Do too many of your sentences start with "there is," "it is," or "here is"? These phrases are usually empty openings because they don't start with a clear subject and a strong verb.

- Do subjects and verbs agree in number? The third person singular subject (he, she, or it) always takes a third person singular verb, which always ends in "s." Be aware that "each" and "one" are singular subjects and therefore take singular verbs. Example: "Each of the girls has written a good paper." "One of the boys is going to the meeting."

- Are pronouns consistent with the noun they refer to? Example: "A person should check his or her (not their) own work." If you want to avoid writing his or her, make the subject plural, as in "People should check their own work." Another point about pronouns: Use object pronouns when they are in the object position. "She told the story to Jim and me" (not I).

It may seem that the Inspector Stage takes about 50% of your writing time. Actually, that percentage isn't far off. Some editors estimate that at least one-third of the total time should go towards refining the paper.

Some writers feel insecure about doing a good job in the Inspector Stage. It could be that they were taught by Miss Grammar Police in sixth grade, who never rewarded for creative ideas but found every dangling modifier and misspelled word. Or perhaps they were taught by Miss Let-it-all-hang-out, who valued free-flowing ideas over the basics and therefore ignored them.

Your personality type may also influence your attitude toward the Inspector Stage. Intuitive writers, for instance, might get so caught up in creating ideas that inspecting for errors seems too mundane. Perceiving writers might not leave enough time for these details because they've spent most of their energy gathering information. Extraverted writers might be impatient to "get on with it" and dislike the isolation that inspecting for details requires. And feeling writers might feel so overwhelmed or defeated at the thought of finding mistakes that they will avoid looking for them.

To begin editing, concentrate on the areas that come most naturally and then progress to the more difficult ones. Chapter Ten has several tips to help your personality type get started.

Chapter Ten:
Using Your Preferences and Nonpreferences in the Inspector Stage

The Inspector Stage has more to do with left-brain than right-brain skills. It requires working with logical order, focusing on fine points, and using verbal ability more accurately. If you have a perfectionist voice in your head, now is the time to invite it in to tell you what's "wrong" with your writing.

When faced with a final draft, how do you go about correcting errors? Do you send your paper through spell-check, put in a few commas here and there, do a quick check for typos, and then consider the job done? Or do you laboriously change every sentence, never really satisfied that you've found everything?

Some personality types are casual about inspecting, and others may be perfectionists. The key to feeling comfortable about the sometimes formidable task of revising is to start out with the techniques that suit your type.

This chapter is divided into the four opposites that make up personality type: Extraversion and Introversion, Sensing and Intuition, Thinking and Feeling, and Judging and Perceiving.

In this stage, you'll want to draw on both your preferences and your nonpreferences.

Start with your preferences and read over the "tendencies." Then use the "tips" as a way to start revising. When you finish that process, look over the tips for your nonpreferences. (For example, sensing types would try some of the tips for intuitive types.) Drawing on your nonpreferences can be a useful way to make sure that you've checked over your piece thoroughly.

Extraversion and Introversion

Extraverts:
Tendencies
- May be too conversational and enthusiastic in tone.
- May resist sitting down in isolation to revise.
- May submit the piece too soon because they haven't reflected on what they need to revise.
- May include too much breadth rather than depth.
- May be too dependent on others' feedback.

Tips:
- Let other people read the final draft and then talk with them about it; as you talk about your paper, you can usually determine for yourself those areas that need revising.
- Look for places that need more development. Try the subordinate paragraph pattern on page 97 to go deeper into one idea.
- Be aware of tone shifts from conversational language to formal language. This shift usually occurs when extraverts are going back and forth between "anecdotal evidence" and evidence from formal studies.

- Proofread actively. For example, use a sheet of paper under each line to look for errors. Doing something active may prevent you from proofreading too quickly or ignoring this stage.
- Practice using active verbs. Active verbs give a sense of forward movement. You'll find a list in the appendix.

Introverts:

Tendencies

- May be too formal in tone because they don't want to be overly familiar with the audience.
- May reflect too much in the revising stage. This tendency to reflect may lead to more ideas and perhaps procrastination.
- May be reluctant to cut because their reflections have led them to such useful insights.
- May not ask for feedback. Introverts are often surprised when they get feedback after the piece is done because they think they have thought the paper through completely.
- May go into too much depth and belabor a point. For this reason, introverts may write long paragraphs.

Tips:

- Read your paper aloud to yourself. You are more likely to pick up an inappropriate tone or awkward phrasing.
- Keep paragraphs short, between three and eight sentences. You can always write two or three paragraphs about the same idea.
- Look carefully at your topic sentence. Cut anything not related to it, even if it is a treasured thought.
- Use more personal pronouns (I, you, we), especially if the piece is less formal, such as a letter or a memo.
- Use a more enthusiastic tone if you're trying to motivate the audience or to sell something. Beginning the paragraph with a question and writing short sentences with active verbs are some ways to connect with the audience.

Sensing and Intuition

Sensing:

Tendencies

- May spend too much time reworking sentences because sentences represent something concrete.
- May not use word choice that engages the audience's imagination.
- May think that the facts are more important than the message and treat them in a literal and methodical way.
- May be too fussy about details, such as formatting, at the expense of larger considerations.
- May believe that correcting the errors is the only part of revising.

Tips:

- Let go of details that don't support your theme.
- Use the sentence pattern sheet in the appendix for revising sentences and correcting punctuation.
- If you have too many facts, use an image or an analogy to illustrate one or two of them.
- Use "Five Quick Ways to Improve Your Style" on page 100.
- Be sure that all your facts are related to the topic sentence.

Write from the Start

Intuition:
Tendencies
- May be too concerned about uniqueness and originality at the expense of practicality.
- May not check for such details as typos or accuracy of facts.
- May write rambling paragraphs.
- May use words that are too abstract.
- May be too concerned with using a varied vocabulary at the expense of clarity.

Tips:
- Be careful not to shift terms. Look for key words in the paragraph and repeat them.
- To avoid rambling, make your point and then stop.
- Be sure that your word choice isn't vague.
- Look up facts for accuracy. You will lose your reader's confidence if a fact doesn't "check out" or "ring true."
- Ask a sensing type to check any detail work that you are avoiding. This detail work may range from finding typographical errors to formatting to looking up facts.

Thinking and Feeling

Thinking:
Tendencies
- May use a tone that is unnecessarily direct or sarcastic.
- May sound as though there were no alternatives to their point of view.
- May write in a clipped, abrupt style.
- May not use enough personal pronouns (I, you, we).
- May use the passive voice too often.

Tips:
- Look for places to put in transitions. These provide "road signs" for your reasoning.
- Check your word choice for preciseness. Since you value accuracy, looking up definitions should get you on your way.
- Use headings to separate blocks of material.
- Use a coordinate paragraph pattern when you need to highlight material. Bullets and lists help you and your reader see what's important.
- Check your sentences for "be" verbs. "Five Quick Ways to Improve Your Style" on page 100 should help you weed out the passive voice.
- Be aware that your tone may sound too definite. Put in some qualifiers, such as "perhaps" or "usually" to show that there may be some exceptions to your point of view.

Feeling:
Tendencies
- May be reluctant to share the piece because of the fear of harsh feedback.
- May have trouble with clarity of thought.
- May neglect to define terms.
- May use too many qualifiers (perhaps, maybe, might) because of their reluctance to take a stand.
- May write in a subjective or personal tone even when the piece is a factual report.

Tips:

- Let a trusted colleague, friend, or family member read your piece. Ask them to point out places where it isn't clear.
- Underline all your qualifiers and take out as many as you can.
- Recognize that part of pleasing your audience is communicating effectively. Check the sentence pattern sheet in the appendix for ways to subordinate less important material and highlight important points (patterns #6 and #7 on page 129).
- Look for ways to make your sentences flow more gracefully. The information on parallelism and transitions should help.
- Consider your audience's level of knowledge and then define the terms that would help them understand the information.
- Check for consistency of argument.

Judging and Perceiving

Judging:

Tendencies

- May set up a planned, systematic, organized approach to revising.
- May believe in "work first, play later."
- May resist changing their writing.
- May lose patience with the piece by this stage.
- May not use enough conditionals or qualifiers.

Tips:

- Use the checklist on page 104 at the end of Chapter Nine; check off the items as you finish.
- Use a systematic approach to help you proofread, such as placing a sheet of paper under each line.
- Check sentence variety by using the sentence pattern sheet in the appendix. Plan to have two complex sentences and one compound sentence per group of ten sentences. Complex sentences, especially, raise the level of sophistication of your piece.
- Read your conclusion against the introduction to see if the piece has delivered what it has promised.
- Add a qualifier every now and then, especially if you're also a thinking type.
- Ask a friend with the perceiving preference to check for completeness. In your drive toward closure, you may have overlooked something vital.

Perceiving:

Tendencies

- May be too wordy or use too many clauses and qualifiers.
- May see so many needed changes that they feel overwhelmed.
- May prefer a random approach to revising.
- May believe that work and play should coexist.
- May have trouble writing conclusions.
- May revise up until the last minute and still not be satisfied.

Tips:

- Go through the paper randomly to see how many mechanical errors you can spot.
- Use "Five Quick Ways to Improve Your Style" on page 100 to weed out wordy phrases and unnecessary clauses.

Write from the Start

- Set aside a certain amount of time to revise. Then reward yourself for completing your task.
- Look through the piece for clues that will lead you toward writing a conclusion. Highlight in yellow those areas that are repeated or are particularly insightful. Ask questions such as, "What was the most interesting or surprising thing I learned?"
- Recognize that your piece is probably too long. Ask a friend with the judging preference to help you cut.

Whole Type Prescriptions

You've just seen how the individual scales can affect the way you revise. But "whole type" can be an even more useful guide. For example, an extravert with sensing and thinking preferences combined with judging (ESTJ) will be very different from an extravert with sensing and feeling preferences combined with perceiving (ESFP), even though they share extraversion and sensing. To see how the combination of letters might influence the Inspector Stage, look again at the tendencies and tips for each of the scales (or opposites) that make up your type.

As you go through the characteristics for each scale, you'll notice that some of them overlap. Since both sensing and judging probably come from the left-brain hemisphere, someone with both S and J in their type will write with order and sequence more often than someone with S and P. For example, an ESTJ will usually write a numbered step-by-step memo while an ESFP may write a numbered paragraph memo one time and a conventional paragraph memo another time, depending on the situation.

This next exercise involves writing a "prescription" to guide your type in the Inspector Stage. The prescription will be based on how the individual scales interact. I'll use ESFP as a model.

ESFP: Talk to someone about your writing. If possible, choose someone you trust to be honest, but not brutal, in guiding you to your final draft. Someone known for a harsh or sarcastic tone will only defeat you. Look for sentences with multiple phrases and clauses and weed out the unnecessary ones — or write two separate sentences. Pay attention to sentence variety to avoid a monotonous tone. Check the parts of your sentences for clarity. For example, be sure that the pronoun "it" refers clearly to a noun coming before. Try some transitions to be sure your sentences logically follow one another, and use parallelism to help your sentences flow. Cut any material that doesn't support your topic sentence. Wake up your reader with a vivid image or two. To write a conclusion, look back over your piece for clues that will lead you to your most important insight or "lesson learned."

In the space below, jot down some ideas for a prescription for your four-letter type. (If your type is ESFP, yours has already been done for you. What would you add to it?)

_____

_____

_____

_____

_____

_____

_____

_____

_____

_____

_____

_____

_____

_____

When you finish writing a prescription for your type, jot down some ideas for a prescription for your opposite type. For example, an ESFP would compile a prescription for an INTJ. If you follow the prescription for your opposite type (after you have first followed your own), you will have considered most of the issues you need to for the final inspection of your piece.

_____

_____

_____

_____

_____

_____

_____

_____

_____

_____

_____

_____

_____

_____

Congratulations! You have now progressed through the four stages of the writing process. I imagine that each stage presented its own unique challenges for you. As you turn to Section Three, think about which stage offers the best opportunity for you to develop the skills you need to continue to grow as a writer.

Write from the Start

Section Three:
Continuing To Grow as a Writer

"Conclusion" doesn't seem to fit the last section of this workbook because learning about type and its effect on writing is ongoing. Though much information is yet to come, people doing research with type have made a promising start. Whether you are a student, an employee who has to write on the job, or someone who likes to write for self-expression, type can help.

Gordon Lawrence, author of *People Types and Tiger Stripes*, believes that schools should incorporate type into their curriculum. One way to do this is to move from the "achievement" model in education to the "developmental" model. That is, rather than focus on "standardized outcomes," education should focus on experiences that promote development of the mind and personality.

Writing teachers can give their students a valuable gift by offering writing experiences based on mind and personality. Fortunately, my elementary and high school teachers let me write about my experiences in my natural style. As a sensing feeling type, I was well served by that approach until I got to college. There, I almost lost my love for writing because the professors insisted I write in their more academic style. Perhaps you began to lose interest in writing much sooner than college.

Supervisors would find it helpful to discover their employees' personality types. They could ask their employees to self-select their type based on the sets of descriptors in Chapter One. After determining their type, employees may also want to take the Loomis-Grandstaff Writing Inventory to get in touch with their preferred way of writing. If employees are encouraged to write in their natural way, they are less likely to waste time (and time is money) trying to write in somebody else's style. Supervisors can then guide the employees in final drafts in a more understanding and less judgmental way.

If you are working on your own to improve your writing skills or to rekindle a love for self-expression, I recommend that you take at least six weeks to self-pace through this workbook. Be sure to try the exercises because they will reinforce the skills you want to strengthen.

This section is designed to help you to continue to develop your skills. Chapter Eleven offers an opportunity for you to learn from the masters. The samples in this chapter are by professionals who know how to use many of the techniques you've learned about in this workbook.

Chapter Twelve should answer some lingering questions about personality type. Recognizing that the concepts can be complex, I've included some information to help clarify type. If this workbook has whetted your appetite for type, check the list of resources in the appendix. I have found that learning about type is a journey that can last a lifetime.

Chapter Eleven:

Practice with Writing Samples

This chapter gives you practice in using the concepts you've learned about in this workbook. The samples are designed to show you how professional writers use the cognitive functions: sensing, intuition, thinking, and feeling. For most of the samples, I have captured their essence (rather than use the full piece) so that you will view them as a springboard for your own adaptation or innovation.

Sample One:

This first sample is from an essay describing a lemon. As you read it, notice how the author uses all five senses. Write your own description one of three ways. 1) Follow the style of the author and describe the inside of the lemon. 2) Take a similar fruit, such as a lime, and compare or contrast it with the lemon. 3) Choose another kind of fruit or vegetable and describe it in detail. If you pretend that the reader has never seen the fruit or vegetable that you're describing, you'll be more likely to think of all the details and to use analogies.

The Lemon

The lemon I hold in my hand is an oval, bright yellow fruit about the size and weight of a large egg. Unlike the egg, the lemon is resilient: I can push a dent into it with my thumb, and when I remove my thumb the dent disappears. When I drop the lemon, it bounces a little, though not as much as a rubber ball. The sound it makes is a solid "thud." The shiny surface is pocked with tiny round dents about the size a dull pencil point might make. These dents cover the surface fairly evenly. The surface is slightly oily to the touch and seems to have no taste. Its smell is a little like fresh leaves or grass, with a slightly acid tinge. As I drive my thumbnail into the surface, I see an oily liquid, and the smell is strong and fruity (19: p. 9).

Sample Two:

This next piece combines sensory detail and figurative language. How does the author help the reader visualize the place he's describing? How many senses are involved? What imagery does the author use? As you read, jot down colors and contrasts.

Subway Station

Standing in a subway station, I began to appreciate the place — almost to enjoy it. First of all, I looked at the lighting: a row of meager electric bulbs, unscreened, yellow, and coated with filth, stretched toward the black mouth of the tunnel, as though it were a bolt hole in an abandoned coal mine.

Then I lingered, with zest, on the walls and ceiling: lavatory tiles which had been white about fifty years ago, and were now encrusted with soot, coated with the remains of a dirty liquid which might be either atmospheric humidity mingled with smog or the result of a perfunctory attempt to clean them with cold water; and, above them, gloomy vaulting from which dingy paint was peeling off like scabs from an old wound, sick black paint leaving a leprous white undersurface.

Beneath my feet, the floor was a nauseating dark brown with black stains upon it which might be stale oil or dry chewing gum or some worse defilement; it looked like the hallway of a condemned slum building. Then my eye traveled to the tracks, where two lines of glittering steel — the only positively clean object in the whole place — ran out of darkness into darkness about an unspeakable mass of congealed oil, puddles of dubious liquid, and mishmash of old cigarette packets, mutilated and filthy newspapers, and the debris that filtered down from the street above through a barred grating in the roof.

As I looked up toward the sunlight, I could see more debris sifting slowly down-ward, and making an abominable pattern in the slanting beam of dirt-laden sunlight. I was going on to relish more features of this unique scene: such as the advertisement posters on the walls — here a text from the Bible, there a half-naked girl, here a woman wearing a hat consisting of a hen sitting on a nest full of eggs, and there a pair of girl's legs walking up the keys of a cash register — all scribbled over with unknown names and well-known obscenities in black crayon and red lipstick; but then my train came in at last, I boarded it, and began to read. The experience was over for the time (10: pp. 92-93).

What pattern of organization does the author use in this piece? You may want to look back at Chapter Five. How does the organization motivate the reader to keep reading?

As you read the next two samples, look for the central image in each one. After you read, pick an image that has meaning for you and freewrite about it. You might want to cluster the image to trigger associations.

Sample Three:

From The Place Where You Live

I have known and loved three very different landscapes in my life — the hills and hardwood forests of southwest Missouri where I grew up, the Gulf Coast of Texas where I raised my children, and the Front Range of the Rockies in Colorado where I now live. Each time that it has been necessary for me to leave one home for another, I have been filled with feelings of sorrow, fear, loss, disorientation.

The moon has been a salvation to me in those times of transition, that moon, a nat-ural presence found everywhere, a place dependable and common to all places on earth at all times — child moon, mother moon, marsh moon, snow moon, birth moon, death moon.

The moon, whether a lavender slit in the sky among winter oaks, or bulging and flat-out orange rising from the plains, or marbled blue and setting behind icy moun-tains, is a familiar I depend on. I search it out always, whatever its phase, wherever I am. It is a steady relative, a close kin that binds, a certain link, not only to past and present landscapes but also to those people I love (you look up too) who may be far away from me in places otherwise alien, unknown, foreign, strange (27: p. 22).

Sample Four:

When I first laid eyes on the northwest Pacific coastal island that has become my home, it took possession of me, much as love blossoms between a woman and man. All dimensions of that love can be found here — in the unpredictability of brown bears and the certitude of mountains; the intensity of gales and peace of towering spruce; the glory of unfurling seas and the shelter of quiet harbors.

I have courted this island, pledged commitment to it, sought ways to tighten the physical and emotional knots that bind me here. Together with my partner Nita, I roam over the landscape and probe its secret places. We drink from the island's streams, gather its autumn berries, catch fish along the shore, and hunt deer for venison that provides our staple food. The island becomes our spirit and our flesh.

Every species of plant and animal that lived here before written history is still present; and this — above all — I dedicate myself to protect. Defender of the island, I am its brother: Nourished by the island, I am its child. Wedded to the island, I am its lover. Here my bones belong (21: p. 24).

Sample Five:

The next sample, "Holiday in New Orleans," uses imagery as well as sensory detail. Using this sample as a model, continue to work with the image you chose in the previous exercise, but this time, connect the image more closely to the senses. In doing so, you will move back and forth between sensing and intuition.

Youthful preachers exhorting hoarsely in a futile attempt to save Bourbon Street, forgetting to feed the hungry or to visit those in prison. Beautiful Boys — "the most beautiful boys in the world" — exploited boys, never to know the joys and challenges of becoming men. "Busty Babes" displaying their wares in strip tease exhibitions, never learning the meaning of womanhood. Bourbon Street is a kaleidoscope of color, obscenity, and excitement. Sounds of jazz, the scattering of coins, shrieking laughter, and steamboat whistles. Smells of simmering shrimp, roasting oysters, sizzling doughnuts, steaming coffee, and blooming spring. Sights of artists bending earnestly over splashes of color on canvas, old buggies pulled by bored horses bedecked in a myriad of bright ribbons and bonnets, shops displaying wares to people, people, people of every size, shape, and bend. Flying homeward at twilight, I witness a spectacular sunset as we soar above the clouds. Pink turns to purple, then deep blue, banked by the deep-orange fire of a disappearing sun, storing its warmth and brightness for another day as it snuggles under Night's deep blue blanket. Like the setting sun, I leave New Orleans as I return to the safety and familiarity of a spouse's comforting snore (1: pp. 54-55).

Sample Six:

Anyone who has spent time with animals knows about their capacity to heal our wounded instincts. If we pay attention to their messages, we can connect with their healing medicine. This next sample is a tribute to deer, whose medicine is gentleness.

You are born into this world as small and fragile as a delicate trinket. Even though your legs don't quite know what to do, they gently and persistently lift you onto your feet from the first moment of your birth. As you grow older, you learn to use those agile legs to run and hide from those who hunt you down. You learn how to fear. The fear that I see in your eyes mirrors my own, but your gentle nature has the power to overcome the demons that block the path to love and compassion. When I wound you, deer, I wound myself. When I embrace you, I heal. Like the dappling of your coat, the light and the dark within myself may be gently loved to create inner peace. Help me to learn that my fears cannot exist in the same heart-space where love and gentleness abide (28: pp. 52-54).

Writing this way about animals helps us to use both sensing and intuition — sensing, because we are noticing details; and intuition, because we are relating those details to something beyond the literal. For this exercise, choose an animal that means something to you. Following the example of the model, write a tribute to that animal. (You might want to start by writing an active imagination dialogue between yourself and the animal.)

Sample Seven:

Journalists and politicians often use their judging function (either thinking or feeling) to convey strong opinions. Former Senator Daniel Patrick Moynihan from New York often made speeches and wrote articles conveying his concern about the crime rate in New York City. This short excerpt from one of his articles, "A Cry for My City," shows how the effective use of quotations conveys strong feelings without sounding opinionated.

> "The slaughter of the innocent marches unabated," says New York State Supreme Court Justice Edwin Torres. He's right; it grows worse by the year. There were 44 homicides by gunshot in 1943. In 1992, there were 1,537. Like other New Yorkers who remember a different era, the judge is horrified by the passive acceptance of violence.
>
> New York City Police Commissioner Raymond Kelly recently reflected on those "No Radio" signs posted in the windows of parked cars. "The translation of 'No Radio' is 'Please break into someone else's car, there's nothing in mine,'" Kelly observed. "These signs are flags of urban surrender. Instead of 'No Radio,' we need new signs that say 'No Surrender.'" If more of us shared that spirit, we might surprise ourselves just how great New York, and all our cities, could once again become (20: pp. 375-377).

This next excerpt, from an article titled "Who's Watching our Children" by journalist Bella English, also conveys strong feelings by using quotations and questions.

> Look at the headlines and you'll be appalled: Wellesley High students leaving school at 11:30 in the morning, when they should have been doing physics or French, trashing a McDonald's, throwing food so violently that customers were terrified, babies crying. The place was such a mess that it closed for several hours. What's the excuse? "My Big Mac was overcooked." "What do you mean, you're out of the veggie burger?" Where were the school officials when this pack headed out? What are their parents teaching them at home? After seeing the movie "Pulp Fiction," a pediatrician struck up a conversation with a police officer. "He told me about toddlers being in movie theaters at 2 a.m., of kids being dropped off by their parents early in the day, sneaking from movie to movie," she said. She was also told of parents who buy their children tickets to R-rated movies, put the kids in their seats and leave. Who is watching our children?
>
> "Parents don't understand the dangers," says David Rosenbloom, director of Join Together, an anti-drug and alcohol program at Boston University. "They'll say, 'Well, at least they're not smoking pot. This is naïve and dangerous because alcohol abuse is so much more common than drug abuse." In fact, many of the teenagers get their booze from their parents' liquor cabinets. Sometimes, parents even buy it for them. Who in the world is watching our children? (See "acknowledgments.")

Now think of a subject that evokes strong feelings for you. How can you write about it without sounding opinionated or "preachy"? (You might want to follow the techniques in the above models.)

Sample Eight:

Scientists, who are often intuitive thinking types, strive to make their theories more understandable to a lay reader. They sometimes do this by writing analogies to clarify a complex topic. Identify the analogies in the next two excerpts.

From The Evolution of Consciousness

Inside the cortex are centers of talents. Talent is an unusual word to use but describes brain operation. Most people probably have more of one talent than another. These abilities, moving gracefully or speaking fluently, exist as mental, behavioral, as well as anatomical, units. Each has a rich concentration of certain abilities. If you imagine each of these areas as a patch, the cortex would look much like a folded patchwork quilt (23: p. 133).

From Why the Sky is Blue

We also know that light consists of waves, and that the different colors of light are produced by waves of different lengths, red light by long waves, and blue light by short waves. The mixture of waves which constitutes sunlight has to struggle through the obstacles it meets in the atmosphere just as the mixture of waves at the seaside has to struggle past the columns of a pier. And these obstacles treat the light waves much as the columns of the pier treat the seawaves. The long waves which constitute red light are hardly affected, but the short waves which constitute blue light are scattered in all directions (11: p. 151).

Now think of some analogies of your own that would help simplify a concept. The analogy can be linked to a mechanical object that might be unfamiliar to a reader. You might also consider an analogy associated with an activity or a hobby, such as a sport or quilt-making. If you get stuck, try a cluster to trigger associations.

Sample Nine:

Writers choose words carefully to convey tone; that is, their attitude toward their subject. This sample, condensed from an article titled "High-fiber Diet Fails to Pass When Facing Scientific Test," helps you identify tone as conveyed through word choice. Underline the words that suggest the author's attitude. Which function do you think the author is using, the thinking function or the feeling function? Why?

After tracking the eating habits of more than 88,000 female nurses over 16 years, the researchers discovered that women who ate a high-fiber diet were no less likely, or more likely, to develop colorectal cancer or polyps, which can be precursors to cancer, than women who ate little fiber. Perhaps women have different colons. This was one line of thinking. Perhaps nurses have colons that allow them to maintain a diet of Big Macs and German chocolate cake without getting colon cancer any more than roughage-munching nurses who wear out their teeth chewing indigestible plants. Perhaps all that hospital formaldehyde does something strange to the colons of female nurses.

Perhaps the real reason that a 16-year study of 88,000 nurses came out the way it did is because the three-decade-old theory by British missionary Dr. Denis Burkitt was wrong from the beginning. The idea that coarse, bulky food, such as bran, stimulates and invigorates the colon to the point that all this activity prevents the formation of polyps and reduces the likelihood of colorectal cancer sounds reasonable. But absent scientific research, practically any crackpot theory can be made to sound good.

Americans should remember that it's healthy to take a dose of skepticism when they confront good-sounding, but untested, health and safety theories (22: p. 4A).

Sample Ten:

This last sample, from "Blame Game Hits New Low," also uses words and phrases that suggest the author's attitude toward the subject. Underline these words and phrases and consider which function the author is using, the thinking function or the feeling function.

> For sheer chutzpah, and a few laughs, it was the best story in yesterday's paper. Aryeh Motzkin, a philosophy professor at Boston University, was fired because he sexually assaulted a junior faculty member and sexually harassed at least three students over a four-year period. So what does the good professor do? He turns around and sues BU for wrongly firing him, claiming that the university discriminated against him as a mentally handicapped person. His suit alleges that he suffers from depression and that the medication he takes loosens inhibitions. Once the school was aware of the allegations, he said, it had an obligation to help him deal with his problem. Say what?
>
> Motzkin is but the latest in a long line of people who force their abominable behavior on others, then, when caught, cry: "The devil made me do it!" Drink, drugs, my mother/father/dog, PMS, steroids, the full moon are all to blame. Anything goes in this whinefest that society has become. (See "acknowledgments.")

You might want to use this space to brainstorm about a topic that you have negative or mixed feelings about. List some words that would convey your attitude about this topic.

_____

_____

_____

_____

_____

_____

_____

_____

_____

_____

_____

Practicing with professional writing is a useful way to build your skills. Continue to look in books, magazines, and newspapers for examples of effective models. As you spot them, consider what makes them good models. It may be the way the author strings his or her words together, or describes the characters, or organizes the piece. Write down whatever grabs your attention.

Write from the Start

Chapter Twelve:
WriteType —
Putting It All Together

Carl Jung saw typology as a "conscious mental pathway throughout life." This mental pathway is sometimes called "type dynamics," meaning that our cognitive functions interact with one another in a developmental pattern, sometimes based on our age. Type, then, can be used as a developmental pathway for conscious growth as we mature. Becoming aware of type dynamics can also help us to continue to grow and mature as writers.

Jung viewed the dominant function as taking the lead in our journey of conscious growth because it is the most trusted part of the personality. During childhood, we develop most of the skills associated with that function. If our caretakers, including our teachers, push us off our path, we will have to spend much energy getting back on it. The dominant function must be clear and trustworthy so that we then have the psychic energy to develop the other functions. The same is true for the dominant's role in the writing process: the dominant takes the lead and then is "served" by the auxiliary. Let's see how the dominant steers us on the path to becoming conscious writers, and then we'll look at how the cognitive functions interact.

The Dominant Function and its Impact on Writing

Dominant Sensing:
ESTP, ESFP, ISTJ, ISFJ.

An ESTP and an ESFP will both extravert their dominant sensing function while an ISTJ and an ISFJ will introvert their dominant sensing function. How will this affect their writing?

When extraverted sensing types (ESTP and ESFP) are asked to write a description of a room, they will likely look over the entire space in no particular order. They may describe the colors or tell how many pictures are on the wall, but they are not likely to focus on one in particular. If there are many sensory details in the room, extraverted sensing types can be overwhelmed by the stimulation. These types tend to take a sweeping look around the room and see details in context of the whole environment. Once they look over the whole scene, then they can describe with more focus or in some kind of order.

When introverted sensing types (ISTJ and ISFJ) are asked to write a description of a room, they will be more likely to describe it spatially — from top to bottom or right to left. They will also tend to focus on one detail and then use their inner experience to relate it to something from the present or past. A picture or a table may remind them of one they saw in a childhood setting, and then they will describe the room from this perspective. Introverted sensing types often have a knack for describing sights or smells in a vivid, realistic way because of their strong internal processing of the senses.

Dominant Intuition:
ENTP, ENFP, INTJ, INFJ.

Extraverted intuitive types (ENTP and ENFP) will see all the possibilities in the room. They will likely notice the harmony of the space and the way colors go together. Connections and associations will also interest the extraverted intuitive type: a person in a picture might resemble a character from a book or movie, and from that connection, a story might start to form. This type is not likely to focus on one object or to order their information because the fun is in what they can create from their imaginations.

Introverted intuitive types (INTJ and INFJ) see the subtleties in the room. As artistic types, they may notice that a picture is too high or that the color in the matting of a picture is off. They are likely to notice what detracts from the aesthetics in the room, such as excessive clutter or an exposed coffeemaker. As focused types, they will likely zero in on one object or picture, often one that aligns with the vivid internal images that come up for them. In fact, they may even temporarily "lose" the room to go with internal images that have emerged. These types should be encouraged to record their images so that they can retrieve them later.

Dominant Thinking:
ESTJ, ENTJ, ISTP, INTP.

Extraverted thinking types (ESTJ and ENTJ) like to organize their external world in categories. In describing a room, they would probably first group the objects: lamps, pictures, or types of tables. As analytical types, they might go around the room rather quickly and put everything they see in a "mental box." As decisive types, they might then make a judgment about whether the room is practical, organized, or efficient.

Introverted thinking types (ISTP and INTP) use their dominant thinking function more internally. When asked to describe a room, they may first look for an illogical relationship of the furniture. Usually patient problem-solvers, they may move the furniture around in their heads to create several scenarios according to the problem they see. Like extraverted thinkers, introverted thinkers are analytical, but they use analysis to compare to some inner standard. They may actually weigh the room against itself — what this room could be if only they were allowed to make some improvements!

Dominant Feeling:
ESFJ, ENFJ, ISFP, INFP.

Extraverted feeling types (ESFJ and ENFJ) like to evaluate what they see by external standards. When they describe a room, they will likely see it in terms of what is considered representative of beauty. A dining room table with a basket of flowers or an elegant baby grand piano may grab their attention. They are likely to be struck by tasteful artwork and to be conscious of the way furniture and fabrics go together. In their description, extraverted feeling types may be quite expressive, using phrases such as "a harmonious blend of colors," "an ornate 18th century hutch," or a "magnificent stone fireplace."

Introverted feeling types (ISFP and INFP) may not notice the external details so much, but they are likely to notice the ambiance of the room. If a room exudes warmth and beauty, it may not be because of an elegant dining room table, but because they sense that the people around the table care about one another. These types will tend to write about their feelings associated with objects they see in the room: ISFPs will likely focus on objects having to do with the natural world, while INFPs will focus on objects containing some kind of symbolism or meaning.

These examples have shown how your dominant function might influence how you write a description, which is a more internal and subjective writing task. Now let's see how both the dominant and auxiliary functions (your cognitive functions) might influence a more external and objective piece of writing, such as a memo.

The Cognitive Functions and their Impact on Writing
ST:
ESTJ, ISTJ, ESTP, ISTP.

Sensing thinking types value direct and up-front information, tangible and useful results, step-by-step format, and clear expectations and justifications. How does this memo reflect ST values?

Dear Fellow Employees:

Recently, our department has had a severe problem with employee conduct, specifically excessive absenteeism and tardiness. The absenteeism and tardiness have affected job performance, which in turn affects our department's productivity. We can no longer afford this conduct.

The hospital requires that all employees observe certain minimum standards of conduct. These standards of conduct are described in detail in your handbook, "A Guide for Employees of Charity Hospital and Medical Center."

To ensure that all employees understand and follow these necessary rules, your supervisor will take the following actions when a job is not performed satisfactorily or when standards for conduct are not met.

1) First incident: Your supervisor will meet privately with the employee to listen to an explanation of the inappropriate conduct. The supervisor will try to reach an understanding with the employee.

2) Second incident: The supervisor will once again discuss the problem with the employee. A written warning might accompany the discussion. A copy of this warning will be given to the employee, and a copy will be placed in the employee's file.

3) If abuses of hospital rules continue, more severe disciplinary action will be taken, up to and including discharge.

If you have any questions or comments, you may talk to me or one of my supervisors. My phone number is - - - -.

SF:
ESFJ, ISFJ, ESFP, ISFP.

Sensing feeling types value personal attention, helping and being helped by others, clear expectations and justifications, and building trusting relationships. How does this memo reflect SF values?

Dear Fellow Employees:

I appreciate the friendly and professional manner in which you serve Charity Hospital and its employees. Each of you can take pride in your vital role in fulfilling Charity's need for high-quality service. To maintain this high level of service, it is essential that we all meet minimum levels of conduct. These rules for conduct are described in detail for you in your handbook, "A Guide for Employees of Charity Hospital and Medical Center."

Recently, I've noticed a trend in absenteeism and tardiness. Let me remind you of the actions that your supervisor may take if the trend continues.

1) First incident: Your supervisor will meet privately with you to listen to your explanation of your conduct. Your supervisor will try to reach an understanding with you.

2) Second incident: Your supervisor will once again discuss the problem with you. A written warning may accompany the discussion. You will receive a copy of the warning, and a copy will be placed in your file.

3) If the conduct continues, more disciplinary action will be taken, with the possibility of discharge.

I want to emphasize that you can talk to me or any of my supervisors at any time. Feel free to call me at - - - -.

NT:

ENTJ, INTJ, ENTP, INTP.

Intuitive thinking types value logical analysis, arguing and explaining, problem-solving, competency, and vision for the future. How does this memo reflect NT values?

Dear Fellow Employees:

Recently, we have had a problem with absenteeism and tardiness. Unfortunately, this conduct is affecting our department's goals for the next millennium. As you know, we would eventually like to be the best department in the hospital. In order to meet that challenge, we must all adhere to certain minimum standards of conduct.

These standards are outlined in detail for you in the hospital's guidebook, "A Guide for Employees of Charity Hospital and Medical Center." I suggest that you read that section as soon as you can because there will be a meeting next week to discuss it. Meanwhile, you need to know the actions your supervisor will take if the absenteeism and tardiness continue:

1) First incident: The supervisor will meet with the employee to listen to reasons for the conduct. The employee and the supervisor will come up with some solutions for the problem.

2) Second incident: The supervisor will again discuss the problem with the employee and analyze why the first solutions haven't worked. A written warning might accompany the discussion. A copy of this warning will be given to the employee and a copy placed in his or her file.

3) If the problem continues, more severe disciplinary action will be taken, up to and including discharge.

If you have questions, comments, or recommendations, you may talk to me or any of my supervisors. My phone number is - - - -.

NF:

ENFJ, INFJ, ENFP, INFP.

Intuitive feeling types value creativity and using the imagination, vision, artistic and original expression, and harmony in their relationships. How does this memo reflect NF values?

My Fellow Employees:

As always, I appreciate the good job you are doing at Charity Hospital. Together, we have built a department that we can all be proud of. However, recently I have noticed that some of you are coming in late or perhaps not at all. Let me remind you that this tardiness and absenteeism could affect our goals for the next millennium.

I encourage you to read the hospital's handbook, "A Guide for Employees of Charity Hospital and Medical Center." The handbook outlines minimum standards of conduct. Since the conduct could affect job performance, your supervisor may take the following actions:

After the first incident, your supervisor will meet privately with you to listen to your explanation of your conduct. You and your supervisor will then share your ideas for solutions.

After the second incident, your supervisor will again discuss the conduct with you. A written warning might accompany the discussion. You will receive a copy of the warning, and a copy will be placed in your files.

If the conduct continues, more disciplinary action could be taken, possibly even discharge.

I invite all of you to call me at any time if you have questions, comments, or recommendations. For your convenience, I've included my phone number: - - - -.

These sample memos show how the cognitive functions tend to influence how we approach everyday writing tasks, but some writing tasks may require using the strengths of other types. As you have seen in the Builder Stage, you can draw on these strengths when you need to. For example, if you're asked to write a review of a movie or to rate a restaurant, you may need to use the skills of an extraverted feeling type and evaluate it in terms of what the public might like or dislike. If you have to write up procedures that categorize steps in a process, you will probably have to use extraverted thinking.

As I was combining various sources for this workbook, I drew on the skills of an ISTJ. I needed to use my left-brain to provide accurate information, sequence, and order. When I want to be particularly persuasive, I use the oratory skills of an ENFJ. In other words, I know that I can visit the "house" of any of the other types, but that I live in the "home" of my own type.

Your ability to use the functions of other types will likely depend on your stage of development, which may also correlate with your age. Here's the way it works.

Dynamic Pattern and Stages of Development

Dynamic pattern refers to the order of your cognitive functions: your dominant function is first and your auxiliary function is second. Your third (or tertiary) function is the opposite of your auxiliary, and your fourth (or inferior) function is the opposite of your dominant. Take a minute now and look back at your own dynamic pattern listed at the top of your profile in Chapter Two. You may remember that the small e and i stand for the attitudes of extraversion and introversion and that our functions operate differently according to whether they are extraverted or introverted.

In the book *From Image to Likeness*, the authors talk about the predictable course of our dynamic pattern when nature is allowed to take its course. They call this predictable course "stages of development" (9: pp. 215-248). To illustrate, let's look at the stages of development of someone whose type is ESTP. The dynamic pattern for an ESTP is Se, Ti, Fe, Ni. As you read, think about your own dynamic pattern and how it has operated in your life.

In childhood, generally between the ages of six and twelve, children are developing their dominant function. An ESTP child, whose dominant function is extraverted sensing (Se), will be more interested in exploring the outdoors and engaging in interactive play than sitting still in a classroom. To engage this child in writing, a teacher will get more response by encouraging the child to write stories or anecdotes about an exciting adventure or a humorous experience. If extraverted sensing is your dominant, you are probably curious about your environment and like hands-on learning.

The next stage, usually from about age twelve to about age twenty-one, the ESTP will be developing the auxiliary function, which for this type is introverted thinking (Ti). Reasoning abilities will get stronger and more compelling. At this point, the teacher could encourage the child or young adult to take a stand on a controversial issue or to engage in debates. It might be particularly helpful if the ESTP learns to write out his or her reasoning process step by-step. Introverted thinking likes to internally order ideas and to problem-solve.

During early adulthood — typically from about age twenty-one until around age thirty-five — the ESTP may begin to develop the third (or tertiary) function, which for this type is extraverted feeling (Fe). Decisions will begin to take on a feeling tone. A female ESTP may find it easier to express her feelings since in our culture, feelings are considered "feminine." However, it may be more difficult for the ESTP male to write from his feeling side, especially if he's in a job where sensitivity and compassion are not encouraged. Extraverted feeling likes to please others and abide by society's notions of "appropriate" behavior.

Finally, beginning sometime during the mid-thirties to early forties, the ESTP will feel stirrings from his fourth (or inferior) function, which for this type is introverted intuition (Ni). Because this function is mainly in the unconscious for the ESTP, he or she may at first distrust it. Dreams, hunches, and images may be dismissed as "hocus pocus" until some mid-life situation forces him or her to look at them seriously. At this point, the ESTP may begin writing about the speculative or the spiritual. Introverted intuition feeds on images, and writing about them helps make the images conscious and more "real."

If your type is ISTJ, notice that the functions are in the same order as the ESTP's, except that the attitudes are reversed.

For example, the ISTJ's dominant function is Si. When sensing is introverted, the impressions from the environment will seem more surrealistic than realistic. Reality will be based on vivid internal reactions. For example, the writing sample about the lemon in Chapter Eleven may cause salivation or a sour facial expression in the ISTJ. Introverted sensing types are likely to trust their body's reactions.

Extraverted thinking (Te) is the ISTJ's second (or auxiliary) function. Extraverted thinking likes to organize the external world and classify objects in it. Cause and effect comes easily to extraverted thinking, as does analysis. That's why writing about controversial issues such as capital punishment or abortion may be easier for those types who are comfortable with extraverted thinking.

Introverted feeling (Fi) is more likely to abide by internal standards of appropriate behavior. This is the ISTJ's third function, which he or she usually develops in adulthood. Writing about personal values is important to feeling types in general, but if you introvert your feeling function, you are more likely to be idealistic about personal values.

The ISTJ may develop his or her fourth function, extraverted intuition (Ne), in mid-life. With extraverted intuition, the images are more chaotic or random. Extraverted intuition is possibility-seeking and can read the nuances behind complex ideas or interpersonal relationships. Writers who feel comfortable with extraverted intuition may enjoy writing fantasy stories.

The stages of development serve as a general guideline to show how we can grow within type. Tracing the stages of development doesn't suggest that our path will be linear. We weave in and out of all the functions as we grow, and environment, trauma, and society's expectations all play a role.

Being well into or beyond mid-life (over age fifty-five) doesn't necessarily mean that we can use all our functions equally well. In fact, some people might not develop their third and fourth functions at all. The third and fourth functions simply aren't as accessible as the dominant and auxiliary, which are more in the conscious mind.

Now that you have a feel for the functions in both their extraverted and introverted attitudes, look again at your own dynamic pattern. For example, if your type is ENFP, your dynamic pattern is Ne, Fi, Te, Si. If your type is INFJ, your dynamic pattern is Ni, Fe, Ti, Se. In the space below, write a description of how your dynamic pattern has operated in your life up to your present stage of development. For example, if your dominant is extraverted intuition, you may have spent your childhood playing fantasy games, or perhaps you had an imaginary playmate. You might want to look back over this chapter for a description of the functions and their attitudes as you do this exercise.

_____

_____

Write from the Start

_____

_____

_____

_____

_____

_____

_____

_____

_____

_____

The Writing Process and Writer's Block

As you practiced with the writing samples in Chapter Eleven, you may have thought: "I could never write this way. These are by professionals, and I'm just an amateur." But professional writers go through drafts just as we all do, and most of them have experienced writer's block just as we all have.

While writing one of his novels, Joseph Conrad once sat for eight hours and wrote three lines, which he erased! Franz Kafka experienced writer's block as "having to see pages filled with things I hate." When faced with a deadline, professionals have to write but sometimes can't because their prose feels lifeless and no longer speaks to people.

Experiences like these are messages that we are forcing our creativity. To refuel the creative process, we need to be more receptive, allowing unconscious material to flow in while shutting the internal editor out. Most of us start with the editor, but the editor will always kill our writing before we have it. The first stage of the writing process works best when it involves some kind of imaginative play that helps us to let go of judging our writing prematurely.

As you go through each stage of the writing process, you'll discover more and more about your writing. You'll no doubt find that the first stage uncovers more levels than you may have thought possible. Writing is, in essence, an act of discovering what you want to say — and you can't discover that without first sifting through layers of ideas, thoughts, and images.

When you do discover what you want to say, you then give form to your creation. Putting your ideas into a shape makes them concrete. In this stage, you uncover even more levels by going back and forth between generating ideas and organizing them. As you work with your writing, a central theme or core thought begins to emerge.

As you expand your idea of what you want your piece to be and do, the core thought will also expand. At this point, it may not be enough to simply inform or entertain your audience — you may need (or want) to persuade, inspire, or motivate. In the latter stages of the writing process, you will likely experience the tension of the opposites in your personality. To grow as a writer, you allow these opposites to co-exist rather than fight with one another.

In taking your writing through the four stages, you will probably find that your paper feels more complete. This completeness often results from the conscious use of the four cognitive functions. If you allow for the interaction of sensing with intuition and thinking with feeling, your writing is more likely to express both the conscious and unconscious parts of yourself.

Reflect now on what you have learned about yourself and your approach to writing. For each stage of the process and for each function of your type, give yourself goals and tips that would enhance your writing confidence.

- During the Dreamer Stage: _____

_____

- During the Designer Stage: _____

_____

- During the Builder Stage: _____

_____

- During the Inspector Stage: _____

_____

- As an extraverted or introverted type: _____

_____

- As a sensing or intuitive type: _____

_____

- As a thinking or feeling type: _____

_____

- As a judging or perceiving type: _____

_____

Summary

A wise and perceptive author once wrote that the act of writing involves so many complexities of heart and mind that it cannot be taught, but can only be caught. In suggesting that writing can be more easily handled by separating it into four stages, I do not offer a pat formula that will work all the time for everybody.

I have found, though, that writing involves different energies at different phases and that these energies flow more freely when they are not competing with one another. Writing is best "caught" when writers allow themselves some flexibility while at the same time maintaining a framework for tackling a writing project.

I hope the house analogy has been helpful in guiding you through the writing process. Just as you may seek out or remodel a house to accommodate your expanding sense of self, so may you encounter writing experiences that reflect your expanding development. As writing opportunities arise, you may want to spend more time on the stage that has, over time, offered the biggest challenge.

Knowing about personality type can go a long way towards helping you tap your writing potential. The need to develop the unused parts of yourself is basic to human nature. May the seeds that have been planted here be the start of a continuously unfolding process that helps you blossom into the writer you want to be!

Appendix

The appendix includes nine sentence patterns, a list of active verbs, and a list of resources.

As you work with the sentence patterns, keep in mind that these are basic suggestions to help you get started on revising. Grammar books and English professors may call the patterns by different names, and the ones here are not the only ones available. This list of nine sentence patterns is neither exhaustive nor "official," but is simply a sampling of some patterns that I've found common and useful. If you are a teacher using this workbook in the classroom, I encourage you to adapt the patterns to fit your own model.

Likewise, the list of active verbs is only a partial list. I include them to remind you that no technique can improve your style as dramatically as using active verbs. You'll no doubt think of other verbs as you read this list, but use these to get off to a good start. If you are a teacher, you might have your students add to the list as an exercise.

Most writers need grammar and style resources for editing and revising. The five I offer here are timely or timeless. If you are hooked on personality type, the five resources on type will continue to feed your addiction. After each resource, I give a main reason for choosing it. Keep in mind that there are many other excellent books on grammar, style, and type.

The Sentence Patterns

Pattern #1:

The simple sentence: subject-verb-complement.

This pattern contains one subject-verb combination, followed by a complement and the appropriate end punctuation. It is the pattern most often used for topic sentences because it provides a direct statement of purpose. Here's an example: The employees were furious about the new policy. There is one subject (employees) and one verb (were) with a complement (furious). Here's another example: Jane and Joe wrote the report together. Even though there are two subjects (Jane and Joe), there is only one verb (wrote); hence, only one subject-verb combination. (Report is the complement, or object of the verb.)

This sentence pattern is very common — so common, in fact, that many writers tend to overdo it, resulting in the "metronome" effect. Those of you who took piano lessons might remember that a metronome measures the beat of your piece. It ticks back and forth in a consistent, rhythmic pace without any variety. Similarly, if you write all pattern #1 sentences, you will lull your readers to sleep. Sentence variety is a sure way to keep your readers awake and interested.

Pattern #2:

The simple sentence: subject-verb-complement plus modifying phrases.

Remember that a simple sentence has one subject-verb combination. Pattern #2 is still a simple sentence but with added words or phrases to make meaning clearer or give added information. Example: The annual meeting, held at the Sheraton, ended abruptly. The subject-verb combination (meeting ended) is the core of the sentence — held at the Sheraton gives added information and can actually be taken out. That is why there are commas around it. This phrase is "interruptive" in that it interrupts or comes between the subject (meeting) and the verb (ended). Note that this phrase can also come at the beginning: Held at the Sheraton, the annual meeting ended abruptly. When the phrase comes at the beginning, it is called "introductory."

Here are some further examples of pattern #2 sentences: The employees, tired and discouraged, left the room. Mr. Brown, moderator, decided to adjourn the meeting. Weighed down with paperwork, Jane decided to stay late at the office. You'll notice several key features about this sentence pattern. It gives the reader further information (usually about the subject); the further information can be left out and meaning will stay intact; and the information will be followed or surrounded by commas. Some writers use dashes if the information in the middle or at the end is particularly strong. Example: Jane — a most unusual worker — stays late at the office every Friday. You can also use parentheses around the phrase to lessen its impact: Jane (a most unusual worker) stays late at the office every Friday. No commas are needed here.

Pattern #3:

The compound sentence with conjunction.

You know that compound means more than one. Pattern #3, then, has more than one thought, or subject-verb combination. It brings these two thoughts together with words like and, but, or, so, for, yet. These words are called coordinating conjunctions. In effect, you are putting together two simple sentences. Example: I took a writing course, and now I feel more confident. The first subject-verb combination is I took, and the second is I feel. The key in writing this sentence pattern is to coordinate similar thoughts that, written by themselves, would sound monotonous like a metronome.

Let's look at another example: Joe wanted to change jobs, but he didn't want a transfer. Notice that the two parts of the sentence are so close that written together they provide a whole that is greater than the parts. This is what sentence pattern #3 does: it provides a way to join "sister" thoughts so that the reader takes in the two thoughts more quickly. The comma after the first thought is like a pause before you go on to the next one.

Pattern #4:

The compound sentence with no conjunction.

While the previous pattern brings together "sister" thoughts, pattern #4 brings together "twin" thoughts. In fact, the thoughts (or the two subject-verb combinations) are so closely related that they almost roll into one other. Example: My novel is about my friends; they haven't read it yet.

Notice two things about this pattern: 1) a semicolon is used in place of the conjunction, such as and or but, and 2) the subject of the second main thought is often a pronoun referring to a key word in the first thought (they refers to friends). Because the thoughts are so close, many writers are tempted to separate them by only a comma, but the comma is too weak without a conjunction. The semicolon actually substitutes for the conjunction.

Let's look at some further examples: Jane quit her job; it was becoming too time-consuming. Susan was promoted to president of the company; she plans to start next week. We'll start the project next week; it's too complex to start this week.

Use this pattern sparingly. For one thing, you don't want to clutter your paragraph with too many semicolons, and for another, this pattern loses its effectiveness when overused. But when short "twin" thoughts come together, pattern #4 is a useful and sophisticated way to join them.

Pattern #5:

The compound sentence with transitions.

This pattern is like patterns #3 and #4 in that the thoughts are closely related and equal. It resembles pattern #3 in that the thoughts are joined together with a word or phrase, and it resembles pattern #4 in that it uses the semicolon. The word or phrase that joins the thoughts in this pattern is called a "transition."

Transitional words or phrases serve as road signs in a piece of writing. They direct the readers' attention by showing them how each new piece of information is related to what came before. The list on the next page shows many of the transitional words and phrases available and suggests their uses.

Here are some examples: My novel is about my family; as a result, I can't go home again. My

Write from the Start

novel covers four generations; therefore, I had to do a lot of research. I spent three days in the library; even so, that wasn't enough time.

"Trans" means to move, as in "transport" and "transit." Similarly, transitions move your thoughts smoothly; they are like bridges that take you to the next idea. Whether they are in the middle of the sentence or at the beginning, or even at the beginning of a paragraph, they link an idea with the previous idea. Transitions provide logic and coherency.

Transitional Words and Expressions

1. To introduce an illustration: for example, for instance, incidentally, in fact
2. To add information: furthermore, in the second place, finally, besides, in addition, likewise, moreover, also
3. To provide a contrast or an objection: however, nevertheless, on the other hand, on the contrary, still, conversely, despite the fact that
4. To offer concession: no doubt, granted that, to be sure, it is true that, naturally, of course, I admit
5. To indicate a logical conclusion or result: therefore, accordingly, consequently, as a result, hence, thus
6. To establish time relationships: afterwards, immediately, meanwhile, in the meantime, recently, first, second, third

Pattern #6:

The complex sentence: main thought and subordinate thought.

This pattern begins with a main thought followed by a subordinate thought. Both thoughts have subject-verb combinations, but only the first one can stand by itself. The second thought is subordinate to the first one and is preceded by what is called a subordinate conjunction: "conjunction," because it joins two ideas; "subordinate," because the idea it introduces is less important than the other (or main) idea.

Subordinate conjunctions are particularly useful if you want to establish a relationship between the two thoughts, such as contrast, cause and effect, a hypothetical condition, or time.

Examples: We'll be able to complete the project by October 15th if the viewgraphs arrive in our office by October 10th. The word "if" expresses a hypothetical condition. We'll complete the project when all the materials arrive. The word "when" expresses time.

Because of the relationship between ideas that these words establish, your sentences will be more coherent when you use this pattern. As a result, your readers will more quickly accept what you are saying. Example: I can't come to the phone now because I'm away from my desk. The word "because" gives a reason for your absence.

Pattern #7:

The complex sentence: subordinate thought and main thought.

You'll notice that in the previous pattern there is no punctuation between the thoughts. The reason is that the main thought comes first. However, in pattern #7, the subordinate thought comes first, so a comma is placed after it to signal the reader that the main thought is to come. Also, if you read it aloud, there is a pause when the subordinate thought comes first but not when it comes last.

Use this pattern when you want to stress the idea in the subordinate thought. Suppose, for example, you want to stress a time change. Example: Since the time for the meeting has been changed to 10:00, we will delay lunch until 1:00. If you wanted to stress the delay in the lunch hour, you might want to write the sentence this way: We will delay lunch until 1:00 since the time for the meeting has been changed to 10:00. Putting information first draws attention to it. Since you are the writer, you decide what information you want to emphasize.

Write from the Start

Subordinate Words

because, when, if, unless, until, since, while, before, after, as, as soon as, although, even though

Pattern #8:

The list.

Many writers, especially in the business world, like the efficiency of using lists. They help the reader to see the important information quickly. Lists are sometimes in a sentence, as in the following example. You'll need to bring the following supplies: notebook, pen, folders, and paper. Some lists are better written in block form, such as in this example.

Tomorrow's meeting will include the following information:

- budget
- retreat date
- new staff
- policy change.

Notice that a colon follows a complete, not a partial, statement. A colon is a strong mark, almost as strong as a period. It says "stop" rather than "pause." That is why the material preceding it must be a complete sentence. Here's an example of an incorrect use of the colon: On the picnic, we will take: hotdogs, chips, and drinks. You do not need a colon here because you are not setting the list apart from the main thought. (Hotdogs, chips, and drinks are the objects in this sentence.) Use the colon sparingly, only for material that should obviously be set apart from the sentence or highlighted in block form.

Pattern #9:

The quotation.

Sometimes we have to use words directly — a substitute won't do. Perhaps no other way can say it exactly as the original, or you are writing dialogue in a personal essay. One point to remember is this: quotation marks go outside periods and commas. Example: "Get a job," the exasperated mother said to her grown son. This rule is true even if there is a partial quote. Example: The new policy stated that there will be "restricted and limited parking."

Quotations are an effective way to get the reader's attention; however, if used too frequently, they are like too much chatter. You don't want to tire your reader by using too many quotations, but now and then, just the right quotation will get just the right attention.

When you have learned how to write a variety of sentence patterns, you will have mastered several other skills: how to punctuate, how to show relationships between thoughts, and how to provide interest for the reader. Keep these patterns at your fingertips when you revise and edit your sentences.

Write from the Start

Active Verbs

Motion

amble	bounce	bustle	cavort	clomp	crawl	dart
dash	drift	flit	gallop	glide	hop	inch
leap	prance	meander	saunter	shuffle	squirm	

Expression

announce	assert	babble	banter	bicker	blabber	blurt
chat	command	comment	confide	declare	echo	express
harp	hesitate	interrupt	invoke	pontificate	rehash	

Direction

advance	approach	ascend	back-pedal	back-track	bypass	circle
continue	converge	crisscross	deviate	emerge	fade	gravitate
gyrate	hightail it	immigrate	hang back	head out	hunker down	

Resources

For editing and revising:

1. Strunk and White. *The Elements of Style*. New York: MacMillan Publishing, 1979. Concise and pithy, this resource can improve your style quickly and painlessly.

2. Houp and Pearsall. *Reporting Technical Information*. 7th Edition. New York: MacMillan Publishing, 1992. This resource for the business world is thorough with excellent visuals.

3. Maggio, Rosalie. *How to Say It: Choice Words, Phrases, Sentences and Paragraphs for Every Situation*. Englewood Cliffs, New Jersey: Prentice Hall, 1990. This resource adapts the English language to particular situations.

4. *REA's Handbook of English Grammar, Style, and Writing. Other Crafting Techniques*. Piscataway, New Jersey: Research and Education Association, 1995. This handbook is particularly useful for crafting effective sentences and improving your style.

5. The Grammar Slammer Software Series. *Grammar Slammer for Wordperfect*. Unlike the typical grammar checker that gives more questions than answers, this one gives solutions. Grammar Slammer is written in the Windows Help format and includes macros you can use to access the program from within Wordperfect. It's also available in other software programs.

For personality type:

1. Kroeger, Otto and Janet Thuesen. *Type Talk*. New York: Dell Publishing, 1988. I like the set of profiles in this resource.

2. Kroeger, Otto and Janet Thuesen. *Type Talk at Work*. New York: Delacorte Press, 1992. In this resource, the authors have adapted their set of profiles to the workplace.

3. Keirsey, David. *Please Understand Me II*. Del Mar, CA: Prometheus Nemesis Book Company, 1998. This is a good resource for learning how temperament relates to type.

4. Thompson, Henry L. *Jung's Function-Attitudes Explained*. Watkinsville, GA: Wormhole Publishing, 1996. The author has done an outstanding job of clarifying the cognitive functions and their attitudes.

5. Pearman, Roger and Sarah Albritton. *I'm Not Crazy, I'm Just Not You*. Palo Alto, CA: Davies-Black Publishing, 1997. This has been a very successful resource for using type in the business world.

References

1. Buie, Lillian. "Holiday in New Orleans." *The Teaching of Writing*. New York: Carlton Press, 1983. (Reprinted by permission.)

2. Cooper-Marcus, Claire. *House as a Mirror of Self: Exploring the Deeper Meaning of Home*. Berkley, CA: Conari Press, 1995.

3. Csikszentmihalyi, Mihaly. *Creativity: Flow and the Psychology of Discovery and Invention*. NY: HarperCollins Publishers, 1996.

4. DiTiberio, John K., and George H. Jensen. "Personality and Individual Writing Processes." *College Composition and Communication*. Vol. 35, No. 3 (1984): 285-297.

5. DiTiberio, John K., and George H. Jensen. *Writing and Personality: Finding Your Voice, Your Style, Your Way*. Palo Alto, CA: Davies-Black, 1995.

6. Elbow, Peter. *Writing with Power: Techniques for Mastering the Writing Process*. Oxford, England and NY: Oxford University Press, 1981.

7. Flowers, Betty S. "Madman, Architect, Carpenter, Judge: Roles and the Writing Process." *Language Arts*. Vol. 58, No. 7 (1981): 834-36.

8. Goldberg, Natalie. *Wild Mind: Living the Writer's Life*. NY: Bantam Books, 1990.

9. Grant, Harold W., Magdala Thompson and Thomas E. Clarke. *From Image to Likeness: A Jungian Path in the Gospel Journey*. NY: Paulist Press, 1983.

10. Highet, Gilbert. *Talents and Geniuses*. NY: Oxford University Press, 1957. (Copyright © 1957 by Gilbert Highet. Reprinted by permission of Curtis Brown, Ltd.)

11. Jeans, Sir James. From "Why the Sky is Blue." *Reporting Technical Information*. 7th ed. Ed. Kenneth W. Houp and Thomas E. Pearsall. NY: MacMillan Publishing, 1992. 151.

12. Johnson, Robert. *Inner Work*. NY: Harper San Francisco, 1986.

13. Kilpatrick, James J. *The Writer's Art*. Kansas City and New York: Andrews, McMeel, & Parker, 1984.

14. Lamott, Anne. *Bird by Bird*. NY: Pantheon Books, 1994.

15. Lowen, Walter. "Data Capacity." *The Type Reporter*. Vol. 3, Nos. 3-4 (1988): 1-3.

16. Lowen, Walter. "Type and the Brain." *The Type Reporter*. Vol. 3, No. 1 (1987): 1-20.

17. Mangelsdorf, Kate, and Evelyn Posey. *Your Choice: A Basic Writing Guide with Readings*. NY: St. Martin's Press, 1997.

18. Moore, Thomas. *Re-enchantment of Everyday Life*. NY: HarperCollins, 1996.

19. Morgan, Fred. Excerpt from "The Lemon." *Here and Now II: An Approach to Writing Through Perception*. 2nd Edition. NY: Harcourt, Brace and Jovanovich, 1972. (Reprinted by permission of the publisher.)

20. Moynihan, Daniel Patrick. "A Cry for My City." *Your Choice: A Basic Writing Guide with Readings*. Ed. Kate Mangelsdorf and Evelyn Posey. NY: St. Martin's Press, 1997. 375-377.

21. Nelson, Richard. "The Place Where You Live." *Orion*. Spring, 1995. (Reprinted by permission. This article first appeared in *Orion*, 195 Main Street, Great Barrington, MA 01230.)

22. Nethaway, Roland. "High-Fiber Diet Fails to Pass When Facing Scientific Test." *The Chapel Hill Herald*. 23 January 1999: A4. (Reprinted by permission.)

23. Ornstein, Robert. *The Evolution of Consciousness*. NY: Prentice Hall Press, 1991.

24. Reynolds, Mark. "Making Freewriting More Productive." *College Composition and Communication*. Vol. 39. (1988): 81-82.

25. Rico, Gabriel Lusser. *Writing the Natural Way: Using Right-Brain Techniques to Release Your Expressive Powers*. Los Angeles: J.P. Tarcher, 1983.

26. Riordan, Daniel G., and Steven E. Pauley. *Technical Report Writing Today*. 6th ed. Boston: Houghton Mifflin, 1996.

27. Rogers, Pattiann. "The Place Where You Live." *Orion*. Spring, 1995. (Reprinted by permission. This article first appeared in *Orion*, 195 Main Street, Great Barrington, MA 01230.)

28. Sams, Jamie, and David Carson. *Medicine Cards: The Discovery of Power Through the Ways of Animals*. Santa Fe, NM: Bear & Co., 1988.

29. Thompson, Henry L. *Jung's Function-Attitudes Explained*. Watkinsville, GA: Wormhole Publishing, 1996.

30. Vaughan, Frances E. *Awakening Intuition*. NY: Doubleday, 1979.

Notes

_____

_____

_____

_____

_____

_____

_____

_____

_____

_____

_____

_____

_____

_____

_____

_____

_____

_____

_____

_____

_____

_____

_____

Notes

Notes

Notes

_____

_____

_____

_____

_____

_____

_____

_____

_____

_____

_____

_____

_____

_____

_____

_____

_____

_____

_____

_____

_____

_____

_____

_____

Write from the Start